INTRODUCTORY PHONETICS AND PHONOLOGY

A Workbook Approach

INTRODUCTORY PHONETICS AND PHONOLOGY

A Workbook Approach

Linda I. House

State University of New York
Geneseo, New York

CRC Press
Taylor & Francis Group
Boca Raton London New York

CRC Press is an imprint of the
Taylor & Francis Group, an informa business

Cover design by Kathryn Houghtaling Lacey

Library of Congress Cataloging-in-Publication Data

House, Linda I.
    Introductory phonetics and phonology : a workbook approach / by Linda I. House.
    p. cm.
    Includes bibliographical references and index.
    ISBN 0-8058-2068-X (pbk. : alk. paper)
    1. Grammar. Comparative and general—Phonology. 2. Phonetics. I. Title.
P217.H66   1998
414—dc21   97-34965

Reprinted 2009 by CRC Press

CRC Press
6000 Broken Sound Parkway, NW
Suite 300, Boca Raton, FL 33487
270 Madison Avenue
New York, NY 10016
2 Park Square, Milton Park
Abingdon, Oxon OX14 4RN, UK

Books published by Lawrence Erlbaum Associates are printed
on acid-free paper, and their bindings are chosen for strength and durability.

10 9 8 7 6 5 4

In Dedication

To my husband, Tom, and my daughters, Amy and Alison—
You are the wind beneath my wings!!

Contents

Preface

This workbook is designed to be practical with a goal of teaching a variety of audiences how to use phonetics as a viable link between the ever-changing spoken and written word. A course in phonetics for the speech/language pathologist has three main purposes. First, the course is designed to teach the normal processes of how sounds are formed and their relation to language development. Second, the course should look at the remediation process and how phonetics can be used for speech correction. Finally, the course should teach the importance of listening skills and how a cultivated ear is the key to success in the therapy process.

The International Phonetic Alphabet (IPA) is a superior tool for learning the correct pronunciation of a given word. For this reason, it is a necessary tool for not only speech/language pathologists but for linguists, media personnel, individuals learning English as a second language (ESL), and others interested in correct pronunciation.

This text focuses on the presentation of broad transcription for all audiences; however, because of the intricate nature of the English language, some narrow transcription symbols are introduced. In my opinion, the use of selected narrow transcription symbols in general transcription is necessary to accurately transcribe certain words in the English language.

This workbook is organized into two parts. The first part introduces the student to the IPA; the anatomical basis of phonemes; and the particular vowel, diphthong, and consonant phonemes. The second part enables the student to learn details about specific phonemes, the concepts of stress at the word and sentence levels, narrow transcription, pronunciation influences, and dialects. Finally, a series of appendixes explaining historical perspectives are included for reference.

ACKNOWLEDGMENTS

I would like to thank the following people:

Robin Weisberg, Book Production Manager at Lawrence Erlbaum Associates, for her time, efforts, and the patience to see this text to completion.

Dr. George Herman, my mentor, who helped me start the process of understanding phonetics 20 years ago.

Dr. Nicholas Schiavetti for chairing the department while I was on sabbatical and for unending encouragement, support, loyalty, and friendship through the years.

Dr. Dale Metz for preparing the spectrograms and, along with his wife Wendy, for being "true friends."

Dr. Robert E. Owens, Jr., Terry Book, and Linda Robinson for professional and personal advice, support, and friendship.

Carol Monteleone, my retired secretary, for helping me start this process, and Brenda Johnston and Joan Schwartz, my current administrative assistants, for helping me complete it. It is your "low profile" work that helped make this possible.

Linda Robinson, Mary Pesarchick, Lori Book, and Linda Payne, for using the manuscript in several classes and providing input.

To all the full-time and part-time faculty in the department for making the workplace enjoyable, productive, and professional.

To my mother who instilled in me at an earlier age the idea that I could accomplish anything to which I set my mind.

To my sisters Jean, Teresa, and Alicia and their families who have consistently supported me in the past years.

To my husband Tom and daughters Amy and Alison—you are what life is all about!!!

—*Linda I. House*

PART I

UNDERSTANDING PHONETICS AND PHONOLOGY

Chapter 1

The Basis of Phonetics
and Phonology

Success in mastering any language requires knowledge in speaking, reading, and writing the language. The speaking component requires the understanding and use of correct pronunciation, emphasis, and syntactic patterns. The written component requires mastery of the alphabet, spelling, and the ability to write, print, or type the pattern.

Very early in the learning process, English-language speakers become keenly aware of the language's lack of sound to symbol correspondence. Any young child studying the alphabet can point out that *cat* starts with the letter c that sounds like a /k/ and the word *race* ends in the letters ce but sounds like an /s/.

In order to help speech/language pathologists, linguists, media personnel, individuals learning English as a second language (ESL) and others interested in correct pronunciation the **International Phonetic Alphabet (IPA)** was devised.

INTERNATIONAL PHONETIC ALPHABET

In 1886, a group of phoneticians from France, Germany, Britain, and Denmark met to discuss the adoption of a universal system of pronunciation. The IPA based on an alphabet written by British phonetician Henry Sweet, represented the first successful attempt to systemize the pronunciation of speech sounds across most languages.

The IPA provides the user with a universally accepted symbol for each of the speech sounds. The IPA is phonetic, not phonemic in design. In other words, a particular symbol is used to represent the pronunciation of a speech sound, not to delineate a change in meaning. Linguistically significant, the IPA symbols summarize present linguistic theory. The IPA has been revised several times over the past century, the most recent changes taking place in 1996.

The International Phonetic Association, the agency governing the IPA, has a system of detailed principles applied to the formation and variation of the alphabet. In its present form, the IPA provides detailed information on vowels, consonants, other additional symbols, diacritics and suprasegmentals. (See Fig. 1.1 for a copy of the IPA.)

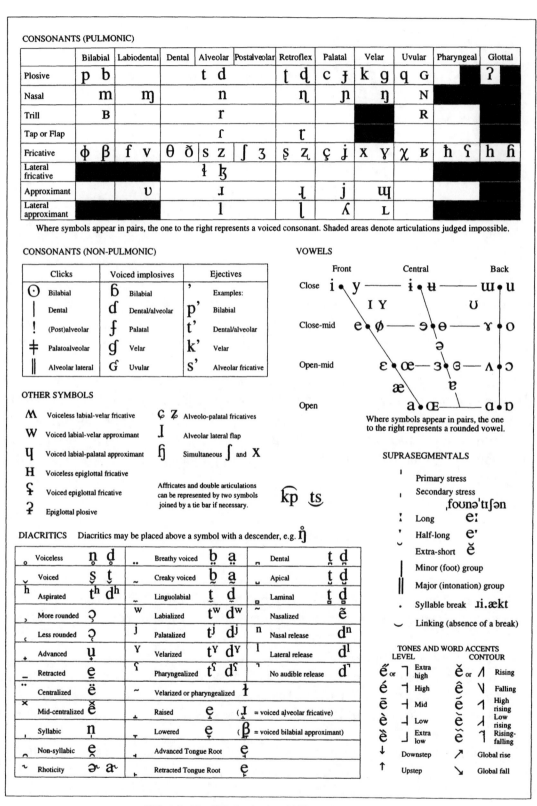

FIG. 1.1. The IPA (revised to 1993, corrected 1996).

4

BASIC TERMINOLOGY

Allophone: The individual variation of the phoneme caused by such factors as position in the word, anatomical structure, and surrounding allophones. Allophones are nondistinctive variations of a phoneme. The use of an allophone does not change the meaning of a word.

Bisyllabic word: A word having two syllables.

Broad transcription: A general type of transcription using phonemes that appear in the vowel and consonant sections of the IPA. This type of transcription is used at the introductory level.

Coarticulation: The influence of the target phoneme on the surrounding phonemes.

Cognate: A pair of consonants produced with the same place and manner of articulation but one is voiced and one is voiceless. Examples: /p-b/, /s-z/.

Distinctive features: Articulatory or acoustic attributes of a phoneme necessary for distinguishing the difference between phonemes. Features are binary in nature meaning the feature is either present (+) or absent (-). Examples: the /n/ is (+) nasal and the /l/ is (+) lateral.

General American Phonetics (GAP): The use of the symbols and markings from the IPA that represent the physical and articulatory aspects of the General American dialect.

Homorganic: Phonemes produced in the same place of articulation that differ in one or more features. Examples: /t-s/ or /p-b-m/.

Loanword: A word that has entered the English language from another language, such as the word *ballet*.

Minimal pairs: Two words that are the same except for the one phoneme. Examples: *hit* and *hip* or *pat* and *bat*.

Monosyllabic word: A word having one syllable.

Morpheme: The smallest unit of meaning in the language. The two common types of morphemes are the **free morphemes** and the **bound morphemes.** The free morpheme provides meaning and stands alone. An example of a free morpheme is the word *boy*. The bound morpheme affixes to a free morpheme to convey meaning such as the plural "s" in boys.

Multisyllabic word: A word having more than two syllables.

Narrow transcription: A more specialized version of transcription using actual allophonic variations and specialized marking. Narrow transcription requires the use of the information from the other symbols, diacritics, and suprasegmental sections of the IPA.

Orthography: The part of the language that uses written symbols to represent the words in our language.

Phone: A single speech sound. Each symbol in the IPA represents a phone.

Phoneme: A family or group of sounds with distinctive acoustic characteristics. The phoneme is used to represent the target or ideal sound. A symbol from the phonetic alphabet is used for each phoneme.

Phonetics: The study of speech sounds in terms of physical and articulatory aspects.

Phonological rules: Rules that dictate how phonemes and allophones are used in the language. In addition, these rules dictate how phonemes and allophones are patterned into allowable syllable structures.

Phonology: The study of the rules and organization of sound units in the language.

Syllable: Unit of the speech consisting of a vowel. Consonants may or may not be present on one or both sides of the vowel.

Vocal tract: The area of the upper body inward from the lips to the lungs that is used in the production of speech. The vocal tract can be open or closed (occluded).

Voicing: The state of the vocal folds during the production of a phoneme or allophone. If the vocal folds are vibrating during the production, the subsequent sound is voiced. If the vocal folds are open or not vibrating during the production, the subsequent sound is voiceless or unvoiced.

Word: A part of language consisting of one or more phonemes and one or more syllables. The meaning of a word is dependent on the entire sequence of phonemes.

VOWELS

Vowels (see Table 1.1) are defined by the IPA using the three dimensions of **height, frontness,** and **rounding**. A quadrilateral space is used to visualize the relationships between the vowels. The **height** of a vowel refers to the position of the mandible (open or close) and the tongue in vertical relationship to the top or bottom of the mouth (low or high). The four variations of height are **open** (or low), **open-mid**, **close-mid**, and **close** (or high). **Frontness** refers to the horizontal position of the tongue in relation to the front or back of the mouth. The three variations of frontness are **front, central,** and **back**. **Rounding** pertains to the pucker or spread posture of the lips. The two lip positions are **rounded** and **unrounded**. It is important to note that all vowels are produced with an open vocal tract and are voiced.

TABLE 1.1
IPA-Vowels Summary Chart

Dimensions	Delineations
Height	Open, open-mid, close-mid, and close
Frontness	Front, central, back
Rounding	Rounded and unrounded

CONSONANTS

Consonants are delineated by the IPA in terms of manner of articulation, place of articulation, and voicing. **Manner of articulation** refers to how the air stream from the lungs is directed to the mouth and modified by the various structures to produce a consonant phoneme. **Place of articulation** refers to the location and constriction of the structures used in the production of a given consonant phoneme. **Voicing** refers to the presence or absence of the vibration of the vocal folds during the production of a phoneme.

The **manners of articulation** (see Table 1.2) in the IPA are **plosive** (the obstruction of the air stream from the lungs followed by a release of the air stream), **nasal** (the release of the sound through the nasal area), **trill** (the rapid fluttering of the lips, uvula, or tongue tip), **tap or flap** (a single tap of the tongue tip against the teeth), **fricative** (modification of a continued air stream from the lungs by the articulators), **lateral fricative** (frictionlike sound being emitted with a lateral airstream), **approximant** (proximity of two articulators without the presence of turbulence), **lateral approximant** (the air stream along the center of the oral cavity is obstructed forcing the emission of air laterally), **ejective stop** (an abrupt production of

TABLE 1.2
IPA Manner of Articulation Summary Chart

Manner	Modification
Plosive	Obstruction of air stream from the lungs followed by a release of the air stream
Nasal	Release of sound through the nasal area
Trill	Rapid fluttering of the lips, uvula, or the tongue
Tap or flap	Single tap of the tongue tip against the teeth
Fricative	Modification of a continued air stream from the lungs by the articulators
Lateral fricative	Frictionlike sound being emitted with a lateral air stream
Approximant	Proximity of two articulators without turbulence
Lateral approximant	Air stream along the center of the oral cavity is obstructed forcing lateral air emission
Ejective stop	Abrupt production of a plosive sound followed by a puff of air
Implosive	A plosive without a puff of air; a weakened version

a plosive sound followed by a puff of air), and **implosive** (a weakened production of a plosive sound without a puff of air). Using the consonant section of Fig. 1.1, manner of articulation can be found on the vertical axis.

The **places of articulation** (see Table 1.3) in the IPA are **bilabial** (using both lips), **labiodental** (using the lower lip and the upper central and lateral incisors), **dental** (placing the tongue between the upper and lower central and lateral incisors), **alveolar** (placing the tongue tip on the alveolar ridge), **postalveolar** (placing the tongue tip in the area directly behind the alveolar ridge), **retroflex** (curling the tongue so that the tip points toward the velum), **palatal** (placing the tongue tip on the hard palate), **velar** (moving the muscles of the velum), **uvular** (movement of the uvula), **pharyngeal** (movement of the muscles in the pharyngeal area) and **glottal** (movement of air through the glottis). Consonants are formed at each of the locations using the structures and functions outlined. Using the consonant section of Fig. 1.1, place of articulation can be found on the horizontal axis.

TABLE 1.3
IPA Place of Articulation Summary Chart

Place	Structures
Bilabial	Both lips
Labiodental	The lower lip and the upper and lateral incisors
Dental	The tongue placed between the upper and lower central and lateral incisors
Alveolar	The tongue tip on the alveolar ridge
Postalveolar	The tongue tip placed in the area directly behind the alveolar ridge
Retroflex	The tongue curled so that the tip points toward the velum
Palatal	The tongue tip placed on the hard palate
Velar	The movement of the muscles of the velum
Uvular	Movement of the uvula
Pharyngeal	Movement of the muscles in the pharyngeal area
Glottal	Movement of air through the glottis

The aspects of **voicing** (see Table 1.4) in the IPA are voiced consonants and voiceless or unvoiced consonants. Using the consonant section of Fig. 1.1, consonants appear as both paired and single entries. By convention, the symbol in the right half of the square is voiced, whereas the symbol in the left half of the square is voiceless or unvoiced. (Table 1.4 includes only the consonants found in GAP.)

TABLE 1.4
IPA-Voicing Summary Chart

Voiceless Consonants	Voiced Consonants
p, t, k	b, d, g
	m, n, ŋ
f, θ, s, ʃ, h	v, ð, z, ʒ
	ɹ, j
	l

OTHER SYMBOLS, DIACRITICS, AND SUPRASEGMENTALS

Other symbols, diacritics and suprasegmental are the three subsections of the IPA used to enhance and further delineate production. The **other symbols** category allows for the transcription of additional sounds not fully represented in the consonant and vowels categories. **Diacritics** are symbols designed to be added to consonant, vowel or other symbols to further describe the phoneme. **Suprasegmentals** provide information on stress, boundaries, timing and pitch. It is important to note that the IPA does not use capital letters for proper nouns, names, or to indicate the beginning of a sentence. Proper nouns and names receive no special delineation. Sentences are delineated through the use of suprasegmental double slash mark at the end.

DISTINCTIVE FEATURES

In addition to classifying phonemes into consonant and vowel categories, they can be classified by distinctive features. The purpose of a distinctive feature classification is to combine the articulatory and acoustic information in order to describe both vowels and consonants. Features are **binary** in nature meaning the feature is either present (+) or absent (-). Chomsky and Halle (1968) proposed the use of 17 features to describe phonemes. These features include: vocalic, consonantal, high, back, low, anterior, coronal, round, tense, voice, continuant, nasal, strident, sonorant, interrupted, distributed and lateral. Features are best thought of as theortical and are not entirely useful in speech production process. It is important to note; however, the relationship between the IPA and distinctive features.

TABLE 1.5
Distinctive Feature Summary Chart

Vocalic: A voiced phoneme produced with an open vocal tract. The phonemes that are (+) vocalic are the vowels, the approximant /ɹ/, and the lateral approximant /l/.

Consonant: Phonemes produced with a constriction of the vocal tract. All consonants with the exception of the /h/ are (+) consonantal.

High: Phonemes made with an elevated tongue position. /k/ and /i/ are (+) high.

Back: Phonemes made with a retracted tongue position. /ɔ/ and /g/ are (+) back.

Low: Phonemes produced with a low tongue position. /æ/ and /h/ are (+) low.

Anterior: Phonemes produced when the point of constriction is anterior to the point of constriction for the /ʃ/, /l/, and /z/ are (+) anterior.

Coronal: Phonemes produced with the tongue blade in a raised position. /θ/ and /t/ are (+) coronal.

Round: Phonemes produced with the lips in a rounded position. /o/ and /w/ are (+) round.

Tense: Phonemes produced with tension in the muscles. /i/ and /u/ are (+) tense.

Voice: Phonemes produced with vibration of the vocal folds. /z/ and /v/ are (+) voice.

Continuant: Phonemes produced in a steady state. /θ/ and /s/ are (+) continuant.

Nasal: Phonemes produced when air is emitted directly through the nasal cavity. /n/ and /m/ are (+) nasal.

Strident: Phonemes produced when air is forced through a small opening causing friction. /f/ and /v/ are (+) strident.

Sonorant: Phonemes produced when the airstream is unimpeded by any structure in the nasal or oral cavity. /m/ and /l/ are (+) sonorant.

Interrupted: Phonemes produced when the airstream is completely occluded at some point during the production. /p/ and /b/ are (+) interrupted.

Distributed: Phonemes produced when the constriction is extended through the vocal tract. /θ/ and /ʃ/ are (+) distributed.

Lateral: A phoneme produced when the air stream is emitted laterally. /l/ is (+) lateral.

PHONOLOGY

The phone is the basic unit of phonology. This single speech sound can take the form of either a phoneme (the target) or the allophone (individual variations of the target). Phonological rules for a particular language dictate both the phonemes and allophones used by the language and the acceptable syllable structures (phoneme/allophone combinations).

Basic patterns used in monosyllabic words are consonant–vowel (CV) as in the word *tea* [ti], vowel–consonant (VC) as in the word *at* [æt], consonant–vowel–consonant (CVC) as in the word *sin* [sɪn], consonant–consonant–vowel–consonant (CCVC) as in the word *stop* [stɑp] and consonant–vowel–consonant–consonant (CVCC) in word *sand* [sænd]. The CVCC pattern is also commonly used to form plurals as in the word *tons* [tʌnz] and past tense as in the word *hopped* [hɑpt]. Other patterns and rules found are discussed in chapters 6 and 8.

PHONETICS AND PHONOLOGY

Phonetics and phonology are strongly interrelated. Phonetics provides the speaker with the sound differentiation necessary to imply linguistic meaning, whereas phonology helps the speaker understand sound patterns, sequences, and coarticulatory interrelationships. Both of these areas are presented in more detail in the subsequent chapters.

GENERAL AMERICAN PHONETICS

Because the IPA is universal in nature and includes symbols and markings for sounds in numerous languages, it is best for the beginning student to focus on a limited version of the alphabet. The primary focus of this text is to introduce the student to **General American Phonetics (GAP)**. Although dialectal variations and various standards of pronunciations are present within the United States, GAP represents the speech patterns used by the media, businesses, and for instruction purposes. The understanding of GAP will provide basic information that can be enhanced with additional study of the IPA.

Review Questions

1. What problem is faced by a speaker who uses the alphabet or the spelling of a word for pronunciation?
2. When was the IPA first used?
3. Who actually wrote the IPA?
4. When was the IPA last revised?
5. What are the five main sections of the IPA?
6. Define each of the following terms briefly.

   phonetics, orthography, phone, phoneme, allophone, morpheme, minimal pairs, cognate, homorganic, distinctive features, broad transcription, narrow transcription, General American Phonetics, syllable, word, monosyllabic word, bisyllabic word, multisyllabic word, vocal tract, voicing, phonology, phonological rules, coarticulation, and loanword.

7. What three aspects are used to delineate consonants?
8. List and define briefly the places of articulation.
9. List and define briefly the manners of articulation.
10. What determines the presence or absence of voicing?
11. List and define briefly the three dimensions used to define vowels.
12. What is vowel height and what are the four variations used by the IPA?
13. What is frontness and what are the three variations used by the IPA?
14. What is rounding and what are the two variations used by the IPA?
15. When are the other symbols or diacritics categories in transcription used?
16. What are suprasegmentals?
17. How are proper nouns, names, and sentences delineated in the IPA?
18. Distinctive features are binary in nature. What does this mean?
19. List and describe briefly the 17 distinctive features according to Chomsky and Halle.
20. What do the phonological rules dictate to the language?
21. What are the five basic phonological patterns found in monosyllabic words in GAP?
22. Are phonetics and phonology interrelated?
23. What do the initials GAP represent?

Exercises

1. Using the IPA chart as a reference, write 10 symbols that you are not familiar with and try to pronounce them using manner and place of articulation information.
2. Considering pronunciation, which of these words do not have direct sound to symbol correspondence?

    psalm, though, hat, ballet, scare, pea, wrist, gnome, tomb, knight

3. List 20 words (not including those listed in Exercise 2) that do not have a direct sound to symbol correspondence.
4. Can you identify the number of sounds and the phonological patterns in the following words? (Remember to say the word aloud and ignore the spelling!)

run	vase
feed	bee
me	key
if	wheat
it	knee
eight	zoo
up	loot

5. At the library, find a phonetics textbook written prior to 1996. Using this text, compare the IPA and GAP symbols. Note changes.

NOTES

Chapter 2

Anatomical and Physiological Correlates

In order to better understand the IPA some basic information in the areas of anatomy and physiology is needed. The information presented in this chapter is brief and intended to provide the beginning phonetic student with an understanding of the intricate relationships of structure, function, and the production of speech sounds. These relationships form interdependent processes necessary for the production of speech. The four processes are respiration, phonation, resonation, and articulation.

Respiration is the process of modifying the air from the lungs for use in breathing and speaking. **Phonation** is the modification of the airstream from the lungs by the movement of the structures in the laryngeal area. **Resonation** is the shading and modification of the airstream from the lungs by the size, shape, and movement of the structures of the nasal, oral, and pharyngeal areas. **Articulation** is the modification of the air stream from the lungs by the various articulators.

The processes of respiration, phonation, and resonation work together to produce the various vowels and diphthongs. These processes are also instrumental in determining the voicing or voiceless aspect of consonants. The process of articulation facilitates the production of consonant sounds. It is important to remember that in addition to their singular functions just stated, each of these four processes have an interactive component effecting the entire vocal tract. The structures creating these processes overlap for maximal efficiency in the production of connected speech.

In the remainder of the chapter, each of the processes is discussed from the anatomical and the physiological perspective. The material is presented in both narrative and outline form for easy reference.

RESPIRATION: THE STRUCTURES

The structures of respiration include the **pulmonary system**, the **chest wall**, the **major** and **minor thoracic muscle groups,** and the **abdominal muscles**. Respiration depends on the nasal, oral, and pharyngeal cavities for air intake.

The Pulmonary System

The pulmonary system is composed of the **trachea**, the **bronchi**, and the **lungs,** working together to bring oxygen to the body. The trachea is a tube of cartilage that connects the larynx and the bronchi and is lined with a mucous membrane. The bronchi are two cartilaginous tubes that are continuous with the trachea and are lined with mucous membrane. These two bronchi subdivide several times forming the secondary bronchi, bronchioles, alveolar ducts, and the alveoli (see Fig. 2.1). The lungs are elastic structures that expand and contract in relation to air supply.

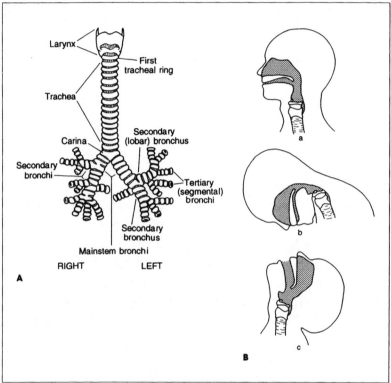

FIG. 2.1. Schematic of the respiratory passage. The upper respiratory tract is shown as the shaded area (from Seikel, King, and Drumright, *Anatomy and Physiology for Speech and Language,* copyright © 1997. Reprinted with permission by Singular Publishing Group, Inc.).

The Chest Wall

 The chest wall consists of **vertebra, clavicles, scapulas, ribs, sternum,** and the **hip bones**. These bony structures create a framework for the respiratory system. The basic framework of the chest wall includes the vertebral column, the rib cage, the pectoral girdle, and the pelvic girdle.

  The vertebral column is composed of five groups of vertebrae including the 7 cervical, 12 thoracic, 5 lumbar, 5 fused sacral, and 4 or 5 fused coccygeal. The thoracic vertebra are particularly important in the process of respiration due to the posterior connection of the ribs at this level of the vertebral column. The rib cage is formed by the thoracic vertebra, the sternum bone, and the 12 pair of ribs. The clavicles or the collarbones form the front section of the pectoral girdle, and the scapula or the shoulder blades form its back section. The hip bones or the pelvic girdle form the bottom of the bony framework (see Fig. 2.2a and 2.2b).

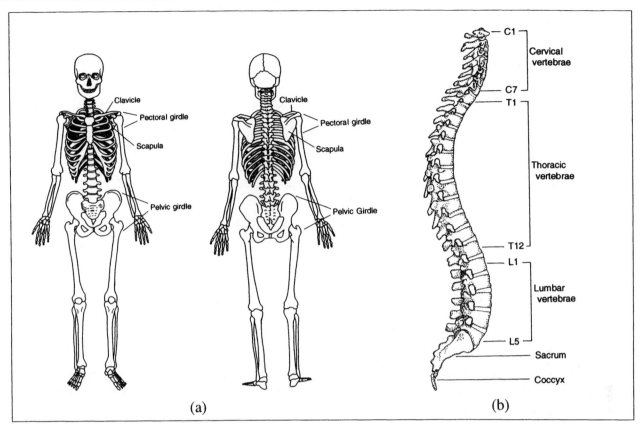

FIG. 2.2. (a) A rib cage and pectoral girdle seen from the front and a scapula in situ as seen from behind. (b) The vertebrael column (from Seikel, King, and Drumright, *Anatomy and Physiology for Speech and Language,* copyright © 1997. Reprinted with permission by Singular Publishing Group, Inc.).

The Muscles

The major muscles include the **diaphragm**, the **external intercostals,** and **internal intercostals**. The minor muscles are the **scalenes**, the **transverse thoracic**, **quadratus lumborum**, **pectoralis major,** and the **pectoralis minor.** The abdominal muscles include **rectus abdominis, external oblique, internal oblique,** and **transverse abdominis**.

The diaphragm is the chief muscle of inspiration, and the external intercostals aid in inspiration and the internal intercostals aid in expiration. The minor muscles serve to elevate or depress the ribs as support for respiration. The abdominal muscles serve the function of compressing the viscera and affecting the size of the thorax (see Fig. 2.3).

RESPIRATION: THE PROCESS

Respiration in the human body involves the flow of gas in outward (**expiratory**) and inward (**inspiratory**) cycles. The flow of gas is the result of pressure changes in the lungs related to the size of the thorax. Inspiration results in the increase in the size of the thorax. The lungs expand in volume and lung pressure is below atmospheric pressure. As a result, air rushes into the expanded lung. Expiration occurs when the size of the thorax is reduced and the lung is compressed causing air to be pushed out. The inspiratory cycle has three phases. The first phase is **ventilation** and involves the flow of air from the atmosphere to the lungs. The second is **external respiration** and is the gas exchange between the lungs and the blood. The third phase is **internal respiration** and involves the exchange of gas between the blood and the body cells.

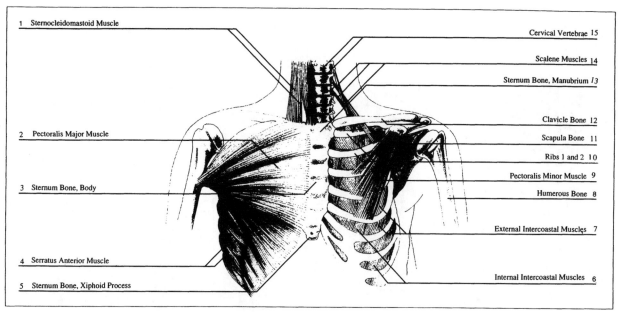

FIG. 2.3. Thoracic respiratory muscles (from Palmer, *Anatomy for Speech and Hearing*, 4th Edition. Reprinted with permission by Williams & Wilkins).

The two cycles vary slightly for quiet breathing, which uses little energy, and for active breathing, which uses considerable muscle support. Specialized respiration for speaking purposes involves the formation of air pressure below the vocal folds (subglottal). In speech breathing, the inspiratory cycle is short in duration and the expiratory cycle accounts for 80% to 90% of the speech breathing cycle. The way the air is released creates various manners of articulation.

Outline Summary of Respiration

A. Structures
  1. Pulmonary system: brings oxygen to the body
     a. Trachea
     b. Bronchi
     c. Lungs
  2. Chest wall: framework of the respiratory system
     a. Vertebra
     b. Clavicles
     c. Scapulas
     d. Ribs
     e. Sternum
     f. Hip bones
  3. Major muscles
     a. Diaphragm: chief muscle of inspiration
     b. External intercostals: aid in inspiration
     c. Internal intercoastals: aid in expiration
  4. Minor muscles: elevate and depress ribs
     a. Scalenes
     b. Transverse thoracic
     c. Quadratus lumborum

    d. Pectoralis major

    e. Pectoralis minor

  5. Abdominal muscles: effect size of thorax

    a. Rectus abdominis

    b. External oblique

    c. Internal oblique

    d. Transverse abdominis

B. Process

  1. Respiration: the process

    a. Inspiration

      1.) Ventilation: air from atmosphere to the lungs

      2.) External respiration: gas exchange—lungs and blood

      3.) Internal respiration: gas exchange—blood and body cells

    b. Expiration

PHONATION: THE STRUCTURES

The structures of phonation include the larynx and its membrane and muscles. The larynx is composed of four important cartilages and several minor cartilages. The thyroid cartilage is the largest cartilage and provides direct protection for the vocal folds. The cricoid cartilage forms the lower back section of the larynx and provides both a resting place for the arytenoid cartilages and a connection to the trachea. The two arytenoid cartilages are important in the movement of the vocal folds (see Fig. 2.4).

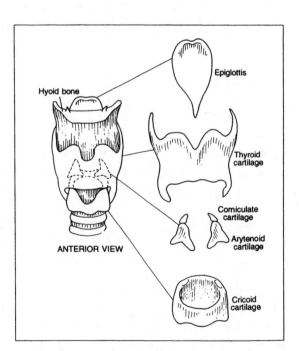

FIG. 2.4. Larynx (left) and cartilages making up the larynx (right) (from Seikel, King, and Drumright, *Anatomy and Physiology for Speech and Language*, copyright © 1997. Reprinted with permission by Singular Publishing Group, Inc.).

The Muscles

The muscles are divided into two main groups called the extrinsic muscles and the intrinsic muscles. The **extrinsic muscles** of the larynx are the **suprahyoids** (**stylohyoid, digastric, mylohyoid, and geniohyoid**) and the **infrahyoids** (**sternohyoid, sternothyroid, thyrohyoid,** and the **omohyoid**). These muscles are

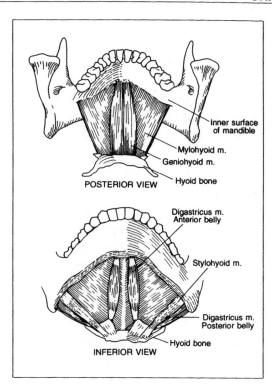

FIG. 2.5. Schematic of the relationship among geniohyoid, mylohyoid, digastric, and stylohyoid muscles (from Seikel, King, and Drumright, *Anatomy and Physiology for Speech and Language,* copyright © 1997. Reprinted with permission by Singular Publishing Group, Inc.).

responsible for movement of the larynx within the neck. The suprahyoids elevate the larynx and the infrahyoids depress the larynx (see Fig. 2.5). The **intrinsic muscles** of the larynx are the **cricothyroid, lateral cricoarytenoid, posterior cricoarytenoid, thyroarytenoid, vocalis, transverse interarytenoid,** and **oblique interarytenoid**. The intrinsic muscles are responsible for movement of the vocal folds and sound production (see Fig. 2.6).

The Vocal Folds

The **vocal folds** are comprised of a **vocal ligament** and the **thyroarytenoid muscle**. The **glottis** is the name given to the space between the vocal folds. There are numerous postures of the vocal folds including open and closed. When the vocal folds are open, air escapes through the glottis creating a friction type noise with no vibration. This posture allows for voiceless phonemes. When the vocal folds are closed, the air stream from the lungs creates pressure behind the closed glottis and causes the vocal folds to separate and vibrate. The open posture creates voiced phonemes.

PHONATION: THE PROCESS

Phonation is the production of sound at the level of the larynx. The process of phonation is not completely understood and researchers are still seeking answers to specific questions about laryngeal functioning. One of the most widely accepted theories of phonation is called the **myoelastic–aerodynamic theory**. The theory can best be explained through the following steps.

1. The glottis is constricted (not necessarily completely closed) by the contraction of the muscles of adduction.
2. Upon reaching the constriction, the air from the lungs increase the amount of pressure against the glottis and creates a negative pressure.

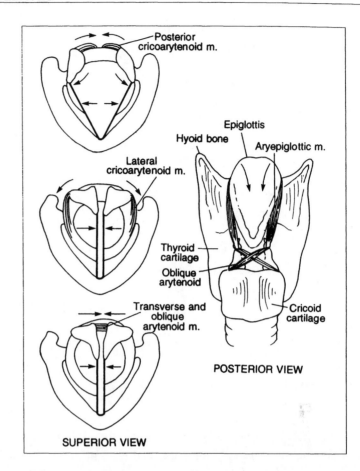

FIG. 2.6. The intrinsic muscles of the larynx (from Seikel, King, and Drumright, *Anatomy and Physiology for Speech and Language*, copyright © 1997. Reprinted with permission by Singular Publishing Group, Inc.).

3. The pressure at the glottis continues to increase as the folds close from negative pressure.
4. The folds are blown apart and air is emitted causing repeated open and closing automatically.

Outline Summary of Phonation

A. Structures
   1. Larynx
      a. Thyroid cartilage
      b. Cricoid cartilage
      c. Arytenoid cartilage
   2. Muscles
      a. Extrinsic: movement of the larynx within the neck
         1.) Suprahyoids: laryngeal elevators
            a) Stylohyoid
            b) Digastric
            c) Mylohyoid
            d) Geniohyoid
         2.) Infrahyoids: laryngeal depressors
            a) Sternohyoid
            b) Sternothyroid
            c) Thyrohyoid
            d) Omohyoid

      b. Intrinsic: production of sound
         1.) Cricothyroid
         2.) Lateral cricoarytenoid
         3.) Posterior cricoarytenoid
         4.) Thyroarytenoid
         5.) Vocalis
         6.) Transverse interarytenoid
         7.) Oblique interarytenoid
    3. Vocal Folds
      a. Vocal ligament
      b. Thyroarytenoid muscle
      c. Glottis
  B. Process
    1. Myoelastic–Aerodynamic Theory

RESONATION: THE STRUCTURES

The structures of resonation are the nasal, oral, and pharyngeal cavities.

Nasal Cavity

The nasal cavity (see Fig. 2.7) is composed of the nose and the nasal cavities. The nose is formed by cartilage and is supported by the two nasal bones and the vomer bone. The floor of the nasal cavity is formed by the maxilla and palatine bones. The roof of the nasal cavity is formed by part of the ethmoid bone. The nasal cavities consist of the inferior, medial, and superior nasal concha. The inferior concha is formed by the inferior turbinate bone. The medial and superior concha are part of the ethmoid bone.

Muscles

There are several small nasal muscles. These muscles serve a limited function in human beings. These are **procerus, nasalis, depressor septi, posterior nasal dilator,** and the **anterior nasal dilator**. The primary role of these muscles is to alter facial expression.

Oral Cavity

The oral cavity (see Fig. 2.7) consists of the **buccal** cavity and the **mouth** cavity. The buccal cavity is the area between the lips and the cheeks. The size of this cavity varies depending on the positions of the structures involved. The mouth cavity consists of the structures in the mouth inside the teeth, including the hard and soft palate. The mouth cavity is lined with a continuous mucous membrane. Although the oral cavity is important to both the processes of resonation and articulation, a detailed description is included in the articulation section.

Pharyngeal Cavity

The pharyngeal cavity (see Fig. 2.7) is a tube of muscle and mucous membrane connecting the larynx and the oral/nasal cavities. It can be subdivided into the laryngopharynx, the nasophayrnx, and the oropharynx.

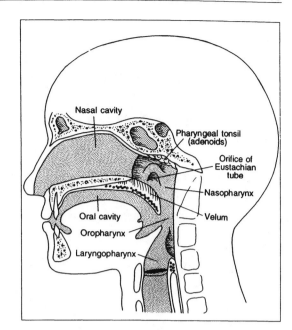

FIG. 2.7. Oral, nasal, and pharyngeal cavities (from Seikel, King, and Drumright, *Anatomy and Physiology for Speech and Language*, copyright © 1997. Reprinted with permission by Singular Publishing Group, Inc.).

The pharyngeal area is extremely important to the resonance of the voice. The actual size and shape of the anatomical structures and the capacity of the structures for variation are crucial to shaping an individual's voice. The pharynx also plays an important role in swallowing.

Muscles

The muscles of the pharyngeal area (see Fig. 2.8) the **superior**, **medial,** and **inferior constrictor muscles**, the **stylopharyngeal,** and **salpingopharyngeal muscles**. These muscles all serve to change the size and shape of the pharyngeal area. The **velopharyngeal sphincter** and **cricopharyngeal muscle** are subdivisions of the constrictor muscles that play a role in velopharyngeal closure and eliciting esophageal speech, respectively.

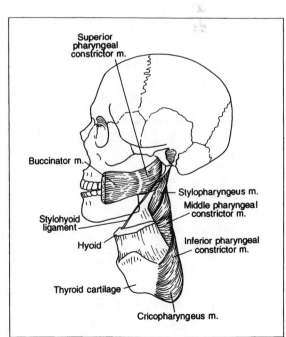

FIG. 2.8. Pharyngeal constrictor muscles (from Seikel, King, and Drumright, *Anatomy and Physiology for Speech and Language*, copyright © 1997. Reprinted with permission by Singular Publishing Group, Inc.).

RESONATION: THE PROCESS

The process of modifying sound from the larynx is accomplished by the air stream moving through the nasal, oral, and pharyngeal cavities. The changing shape created by muscle movement and varying tension of the membranes in the cavities produces the various **formants.** Formants are the overtones or resonances of the vocal tract. Each phoneme has a distinct pattern of formants. The formant of each of the vowels is included in chapter 3.

These cavities are also important for their functions of warming, moistening, and cleaning the air that enters the respiratory tract and aids swallowing. Air enters the nose via the **nares** (nostrils) and goes directly into the nasal concha or into the respiratory path to the lungs. The entire nasal cavity is lined with a continuous mucous membrane and is an important organ of smell.

Outline Summary of Resonation

A. Structures
1. Nasal Cavity
    a. Subdivisions
       1.) Nose
       2.) Nasal cavities
    b. Bony structure
       1.) Maxilla bones: forms floor
       2.) Palatine bones: forms floor
       3.) Ethmoid bone: forms roof and medial and superior concha
       4.) Vomer bone: support for nose
       5.) Inferior turbinate bone: forms inferior concha
    c. Muscles: limited role in humans—effect facial expression
       1.) Procerus
       2.) Nasalis
       3.) Depressor septi
       4.) Posterior nasal dilator
       5.) Anterior nasal dilator
2. Oral cavity (more information will be under articulation)
    a. Subdivisions
       1.) Mouth cavity
       2.) Buccal cavity
       3.) Pharyngeal cavity: provides individual voice quality
    a. Subdivisions
       1.) Laryngopharynx
       2.) Nasopharynx
       3.) Oropharynx
    b. Pharyngeal muscles: change size and shape of the area
       1.) Superior constrictor
       2.) Medial constrictor
       3.) Inferior constrictor
       4.) Stylopharyngeal
       5.) Salpingopharyngeal

B. Process
1. Formants
2. Warm, moisten, clean air
3. Swallowing

ARTICULATION: THE STRUCTURES

The structures for articulation are called the articulators. The articulators are the tongue, lips, teeth, hard palate, soft palate (velum), and glottis. These structures, with the exception of the glottis, compose the oral cavity.

Lips

The lips are the outermost articulator. They are formed externally by the skin and internally by mucous membrane. Between these two sections is muscular, glandular, and fat tissue. The landmark's of the lip (see Fig. 2.9) include the **vermilion** (red area), **philtrum** (the groove under the nasal area), the **columella** (the ridge on each side on the philtrum), and the **Cupid's bow** (the varied shape in the middle of the upper lip). Bilabial and labiodental consonants are formed by the lips.

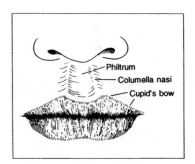

FIG. 2.9. Landmarks of the lips (from Seikel, King, and Drumright, *Anatomy and Physiology for Speech and Language,* copyright © 1997. Reprinted with permission by Singular Publishing Group, Inc.).

Teeth

There are two types of teeth, deciduous (milk or baby) and permanent teeth. There are 20 deciduous teeth that begin to erupt at about 6 months of age and are lost by about 12 years of age. It is obvious that the deciduous teeth are important for both eating and speech. They are also important in shaping the mouth for the 32 permanent teeth and for the production of phonemes. These teeth and their alignment play a key role in the production of phonemes. The permanent teeth are the upper and lower central incisors, the upper and lower lateral incisors, the upper and lower cuspids, the upper and lower first bicuspids, the upper and lower second bicuspids, the upper and lower first molars, the upper and lower second molars, and the upper and lower third molars (see Fig. 2.10). The labiodental and dental consonants are formed directly by the teeth.

Tongue

The tongue is considered by many phoneticians to be the most important articulator because of its great flexibility and its capacity to compensate for other structural problems. The tongue is composed of connective tissue covered by muscle tissue. The outermost layer has numerous landmarks (see Fig. 2.10). The four major areas of the tongue are the tip (the foremost section), the blade (just behind the tip and in the front area), the front (just below the hard palate), and the back (the area below the velum). The dorsum refers to the superior surface of the tongue.

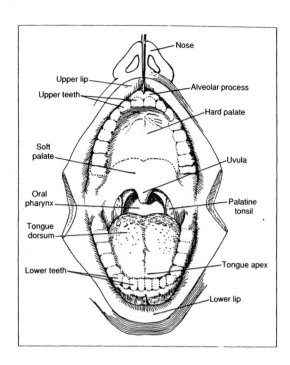

FIG. 2.10. The oral cavity (from Palmer and Yantis, *Survey of Communication Disorders*, copyright © 1990. Reprinted with permission by Williams & Wilkins).

Hard Palate

The hard palate is composed of the two **maxillary** and two **palatine bones**. These four bones fuse early in the embryological development to form one structure. The integrity of the hard palate is important for resonance and as a point of attachment for muscle tissue. The front section of the hard palate is called the **alveolar ridge** or process. Numerous consonants are formed using the alveolar, post alveolar, and palatal areas as a placement.

Soft Palate

The soft palate is locate directly behind the hard palate and is comprised of muscle tissue with a membranous covering. The movement of the soft palate allows for velopharyngeal closure. The velar consonants are formed by the role of the velum in articulation.

Glottis

The glottis is the space between the vocal folds when open. This area is important in both the production of glottal sounds and for differentiating voiced and voiceless sounds.

Muscles

Numerous muscles organized into muscle groups are important to articulation. These muscles are listed here.

Facial Expression. Figure 2.11 shows the muscles of facial expression. They are as follows:

1. Levator labii superior: elevates parts of the upper lip.
2. Levator anguli oris: elevates parts of the upper lip.
3. Zygomatic: moves the corners of the mouth up and back.
4. Risorius: retracts the corners of the mouth.
5. Depressor anguli oris: depresses the lower lip.

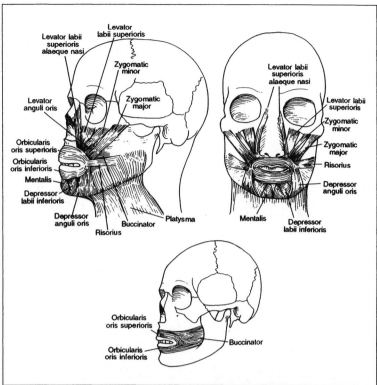

FIG. 2.11. Muscles of the face (from Seikel, King, and Drumright, *Anatomy and Physiology for Speech and Language,* copyright © 1997. Reprinted with permission by Singular Publishing Group, Inc.).

6. Depressor labii inferior: depresses the lower lip.
7. Mental: protrudes the lower lip and wrinkles the chin.
8. Orbicularis oris: puckers the lips and closes the mouth.
9. Buccinator: flattens the cheek.
10. Platysma: depresses the corners of the mouth, depresses the mandible, wrinkles the skin of the chin and neck.

Mastication.   Figure 2.12 shows the temporalis muscle of mastication. The muscles of mastication are as follows:

1. Temporalis: raises and retracts the mandible.
2. Masseter: raises the mandible to the maxilla.
3. Internal pterygoid: raises and protrudes the mandible.
4. External pterygoid: draws the mandible forward, sideward and depresses it.

Soft Palate (Velar)   Figure 2.13 shows the muscles of the velum. They are as follows:

1. Levator veli palatine: raises the soft palate toward the posterior pharyngeal wall.
2. Tensor veli palatine: tenses the soft palate and during swallowing opens the Eustachian tube.
3. Uvula: raises and shortens the uvula.
4. Glossopalatine (palatoglossus): raises the back portion of the tongue and depresses the sides of the palate.
5. Pharyngopalatine (palatopharyngeal): depresses the soft palate and elevates the pharynx and larynx.

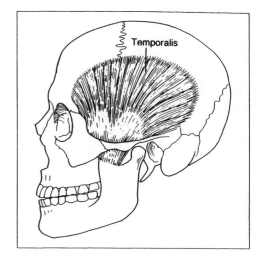

FIG. 2.12. Graphic representation of the temporalis (from Seikel, King, and Drumright, *Anatomy and Physiology for Speech and Language,* copyright © 1997. Reprinted with permission by Singular Publishing Group, Inc.).

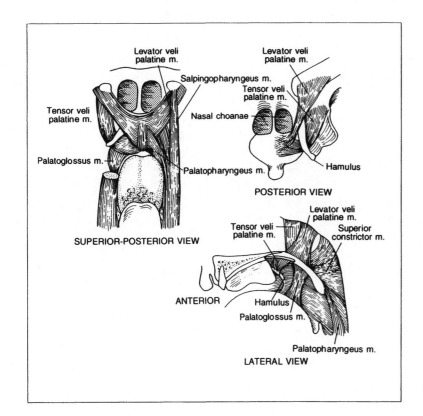

FIG. 2.13. Muscles of the velum (from Seikel, King, and Drumright, *Anatomy and Physiology for Speech and Language,* copyright © 1997. Reprinted with permission by Singular Publishing Group, Inc.).

Intrinsic Tongue.   Figure 2.14a and 2.14b shows the intrinsic muscles of the tongue. They are as follows:

1. Vertical: widens and flattens the tongue tip.
2. Transverse: elongates and narrows the tongue.
3. Inferior longitudinal: shortens the tongue and depresses the tip.
4. Superior longitudinal: shortens the tongue, raises the tongue tip and tongue edges creating a concave appearance.

Extrinsic Tongue. The extrinsic muscles of the tongure are shown in Fig. 2.14a and are listed here:

1. Styloglossus: draws the tongue up and back creating a concave dorsum.
2. Genioglossus: depresses, retracts, and protrudes the tongue tip.
3. Hyoglossus: depresses and retracts the tongue.
4. Glossopalatine: see muscles of the soft palate.

ARTICULATION: THE PROCESS

Articulation is the process of modifying the air stream by the articulators. Plosives, fricatives, nasals, affricates, and approximants are the result the manner of articulation.

Velopharyngeal Functioning

Understanding the concept of velopharyngeal closure is basic to the production of speech sounds. Velopharyngeal closure is accomplished by the movement of the velum, at the level of the superior constrictor, backward and upward to meet the back wall of the pharynx. This movement is used in our language for the production of all phonemes except the nasals /m/, /n/, and /ŋ/.

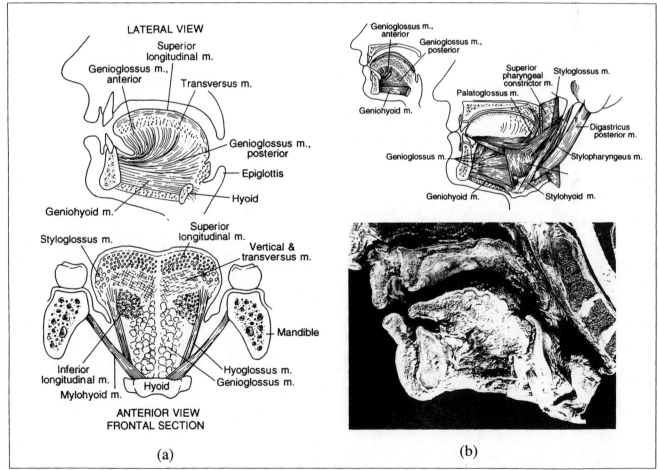

FIG. 2.14. (a) The intrinsic muscles of the tongue. (b) Genioglossus and related muscles (from Seikel, King, and Drumright, *Anatomy and Physiology for Speech and Language,* copyright © 1997. Reprinted with permission by Singular Publishing Group, Inc.).

Tonsil Ring

The tonsil ring (see Fig. 2.15) is a near circle of lymph tissue located near the entrance of the nasal and oral cavity. It serves as a protection system ridding the body of waste material. There are three parts to the tonsillar ring. The pharyngeal tonsil (called the adenoid when infected) is located in the nasophayrnx above the soft palate. The palatine tonsils are locate in the oral cavity under the palatine bones. The ring is completed by the numerous lingual tonsils located in the oral cavity directly on the tongue. The tonsils are often enlarged in children but tend to atrophy after puberty.

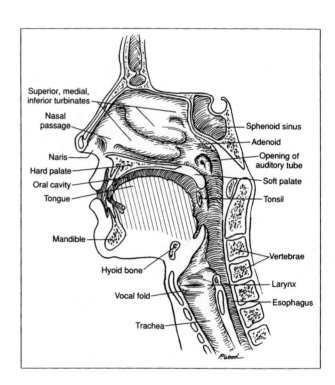

FIG. 2.15. The vocal tract (from Palmer and Yantis, *Survey of Communication Disorders,* copyright © 1990. Reprinted with permission by Williams & Wilkins).

Outline Summary of Articulation

A. Structures: articulators
 1. Lips
  a. Vermilion
  b. Philtrum
  c. Columella
  d. Cupid's bow
 2. Teeth
  a. Deciduous
  b. Permanent
 3. Tongue
  a. Tip
  b. Blade
  c. Front
  d. Back

　　4. Hard palate
　　　　a. Maxillary bones
　　　　b. Palatine bones
　　　　c. Alveolar ridge
　　5. Soft palate (velum)
　　6. Glottis
　　7. Muscles
　　　　a. Facial expression: movement of lip, mouth, and cheek
　　　　　　1.) Levator labii superior
　　　　　　2.) Levator anguli oris
　　　　　　3.) Zygomatic
　　　　　　4.) Risorius
　　　　　　5.) Depressor anguli oris
　　　　　　6.) Depressor labii inferior
　　　　　　7.) Mental
　　　　　　8.) Orbicularis oris
　　　　　　9.) Buccinator
　　　　　　10.) Platysma
　　　　b. Mastication: movement of the mandible
　　　　　　1.) Temporal
　　　　　　2.) Masseter
　　　　　　3.) Internal pterygoid
　　　　　　4.) External pterygoid
　　　　c. Soft palate: movement of the soft palate
　　　　　　1.) Levator veli palatine
　　　　　　2.) Tensor veli palatine
　　　　　　3.) Uvula
　　　　　　4.) Glossopalatine
　　　　　　5.) Pharyngopalatine
　　　　d. Intrinsic tongue: changes shape of the tongue
　　　　　　1.) Vertical
　　　　　　2.) Transverse
　　　　　　3.) Inferior longitudinal
　　　　　　4.) Superior longitudinal
　　　　e. Extrinsic tongue: movement of the tongue within the oral cavity
　　　　　　1.) Styloglossus
　　　　　　2.) Genioglossus
　　　　　　3.) Hyoglossus
　　　　　　4.) Glossopalatine
　B. Process
　　1. Velopharyngeal functioning
　　2. Tonsil ring

Review Questions

　1. What are the four processes that are important in the production of speech sounds?
　2. Which three processes produce the vowels and diphthongs?

3. Which process produces the consonants?
4. What are the three main parts of the pulmonary system and their combined function?
5. What are the structures of the chest wall and what is their combined function?
6. What is the chief muscle of inspiration?
7. What are the two cycles of respiration?
8. During inspiration, how is the size of the thorax effected? How is it effected during expiration?
9. Describe briefly the three phases of inspiratory cycle.
10. What is the primary function of the process of respiration? What is a secondary function?
11. During speech breathing, what percent of the cycle is devoted to expiration? What percent is devoted to inspiration?
12. What is the role of the thyroid cartilage?
13. What is the role of the cricoid cartilage?
14. What is the importance of the arytenoid cartilages?
15. For what are the extrinsic laryngeal muscles responsible?
16. For what are the intrinsic laryngeal muscles responsible?
17. What is the name of the space between the vocal folds?
18. What vocal fold posture creates a voice sound? What vocal fold posture creates a voiceless sound?
19. What is the name of a widely accepted theory of phonation?
20. What is a formant?
21. What are the two main functions of the nasal cavity?
22. What five bones provide support to the nasal area?
23. What are the two parts of the oral cavity?
24. What are the three parts of the pharyngeal cavity?
25. The pharyngeal cavity is very important in the production of what aspect of the voice?
26. Other than voicing, what is another role of the pharyngeal cavity?
27. List the articulators.
28. What type of consonant sounds are formed by the lips?
29. What are the two types of teeth?
30. What is the most important articulator? Why?
31. What are the major areas of the tongue?
32. What are the four bones that form the hard palate?
33. What is the most important role of the velum?
34. What five muscles groups play an important role in articulation?
35. What speech sounds do not require velopharyngeal closure?
36. What are the various types of tonsils?

Exercises

1. Using models or diagrams from other sources, locate the various structures discussed in the chapter.

NOTES

Chapter 3

Vowels

The first part of the GAP studied in detail is the section on vowels. A clear understanding of the vowels is important because vowels are the nucleus of the syllable. Fifteen vowels are commonly used in American English. Of these 15 vowels, GAP uses 13. The other 2 (/a/ and /ɒ/) are used in the eastern dialect.

In chapter 1, vowels are defined by the IPA using the three dimensions of height, frontness, and rounding. Each of these three parameters is presented in detail from the perspective of the physical dimensions (the auditory attributes). It is helpful to refer to Fig. 3.1 while reading the narrative explanations of each of the vowels.

The chapter concludes with a brief discussion on acoustic phonetics and visual displays of 11 vowels commonly used in GAP.

	Front	Central	Back
Close	i		u
	ɪ	ʊ	
Close-Mid	e	ə	o
Open-Mid	ɛ	ʌ ɔ	
	æ		
Open	a	ɑ ɒ	

FIG. 3.1. The GAP vowel chart.

PHYSICAL DIMENSIONS

Vowel Height

Vowel height is affected by both the position of the mandible (open or close) and the vertical position of the tongue (low or high). The four variations used to define vowel height are **open, open-mid, close-mid**, and **close.**

1. Open: Open vowels use a depressed position of the mandible with a low position of the tongue. The most open vowel in GAP is the /ɑ/ phoneme. The eastern dialect uses the /a/ and the /ɒ/, which are also open vowels.
2. Open-mid: Open-mid vowels use a partially depressed position of the mandible with the tongue position being located half way between the palatal area and the floor of the mouth. The open-mid vowels are /ɛ/, /ʌ/, and /ɔ/.
3. Closed-mid: Closed-mid vowels use a closed mandibular position with a tongue position that is located half way between the palatal area and the floor of the mouth. The closed-mid vowels are /e/ and /o/.
4. Close: Close vowels use a closed mandibular position and a high tongue position. The tongue is actually resting on the alveolar ridge. The close vowels are /i/ and /u/.

Close examination of the vowel chart shows that several vowels are not clearly defined using the height labels just listed. In order to provide clear, descriptive labels for all vowels, phoneticians have agreed on the use of the terms **near-open** and **near-close** to describe the additional vowels. The near-open vowel /æ/ lays between the open-mid and open vowels, whereas the near-close vowels /ɪ/ and /ʊ/ lay between the close and close-mid vowels.

Frontness

There are three degrees of frontness: **back, central,** and **front.**

1. Back: Back vowels are produced when the back portion of the tongue is moved up or down in the velar area. The back vowels in GAP are /u/, /ʊ/, /o/, /ɔ/, /ʌ/, and /ɑ/. The eastern dialectal vowel /ɒ/ is also included on the vowel chart as a back vowel.
2. Central: The central vowel is produced when the tongue is resting in a neutral position in the oral cavity. The central vowel is /ə/. The /ə/ is the unstressed version of numerous vowels.
3. Front: The front vowels are produced by the placement of the tongue tip in various positions from the upper incisors to the lower incisors. The front vowels in GAP are /i/, /ɪ/, /e/, /ɛ/, and /æ/. The eastern vowel /a/ also included on the vowel chart is a front vowel.

Rounding

Lip rounding refers to the position of the lips during the production of the vowel. The positions commonly described are rounded—vowels are located on the right of the line forming the quadrilateral—and unrounded—vowels on the left of the line.

1. Rounded: Vowels produced in the rounded position require the lips to be open and protruded to some degree. The rounded vowels in GAP are /u/, /ʊ/, /o/, and /ɔ/. The eastern vowel /ɒ/ is also a rounded vowel.
2. Unrounded: Vowels produced in the unrounded position require the lips to be spread and the corners of the mouth retracted to varying degrees. The unrounded vowels in GAP are /i/, /ɪ/, /e/, /ɛ/, /æ/, /ʌ/, and /ɑ/. The eastern vowel /a/ is also an unrounded vowel.

Vowels

Vowels are plotted in a quadrilateral space. The use of the quadrilateral format allows the notion of vowel space. The vowel space is correlated to the position of the tongue, lips, mandible, oral cavity size, and the acoustic aspects of the vowel production. Use of the vowel chart (see Fig. 3.1) helps facilitate discussion and convey information about the vowel dimensions of height, frontness, and rounding. The chart represents all vowel possibilities. Although the IPA uses a chart for the vowels, these locations represent acoustic measurements and not auditory impressions. The vowel positions are not absolutes. The charting format is important because it allows the understanding of the interrelationship of the vowels. Although vowels can be defined in terms of height, frontness, and roundness, vowels are best described as appearing on a continuum with varying distances between the values.

Vowels can also be describe by the amount of tension manifested by the muscles, the relative duration of the production and the types of syllables in which they can occur.

Tense–Lax

Tense vowels require tension in selected muscles for production and are long in duration. The tense vowels in GAP are /i/, /e/, /u/, /o/, /ɔ/, /ɑ/. **Lax** vowels are produced when the muscles are in resting postures and are short in duration. The lax vowels in GAP are /ɪ/, /ɛ/, /æ/, /ʊ/, /ʌ/.

Several of the vowels can be described in terms of tense–lax pairs. These are /i/ and /ɪ/, /e/ and /ɛ/, and /u/ and /ʊ/. It is common for nonnative english speakers to confuse these vowels substituting the tense vowel for its lax counterpart. In the eastern dialect or in British-English /ɑ/ and /ɒ/ are paired. The /ɒ/ is the lax counterpart. Although there is no symbolization for this feature in the IPA, every vowel can be described as being either tense or lax.

Open–Close Syllables

Open and closed syllables are two common syllable types used in the English language. An **open** syllable is a syllable that ends with a tense vowel or a diphthong (see chapter 4). In a monosyllabic word, the basic phonological pattern for an open syllable is **CV**. A **closed syllable** is a syllable that ends with a consonant sound. In a monosyllabic word, the basic phonological patterns for a closed syllable is **VC** or **CVC**. Tense vowels can appear in both open and closed syllables, whereas lax vowels can appear only in closed syllables. Both tense and lax vowels can initiate a syllable.

Vowel Length

Vowel duration varies depending on the phonemes in adjacent positions to the given vowel and dialectal variations. Some vowels, however, are consistently longer in duration. These long vowels in GAP are /i/, /ɔ/, and /ɑ/. Symbols for denoting vowel length are found in the suprasegmental section of the IPA.

EXPLANATION OF VOWEL PRESENTATION FORMAT

Each vowel is discussed in terms of parameters (physical dimensions) of height, frontness, and rounding; a list of common orthographic interpretations (no attempt is made to include all possible spellings), a comments section, a list of monosyllabic words for phonetic transcription practice, and a list of words written in phonetics for reading practice. All monosyllabic practice words use consonants that are similar in both orthography and phonetics. (The /k/ phoneme is also included.) Because vowels are not absolute values, no explanation of production is provided. This information would be both limiting and contradictory. Each of the symbols is named according to Pullum and Ladusaw (1986).

For purposes of clarity and consistency, all parameters are listed in the order of height, frontness, and rounding. Because all vowels require an open velopharyngeal port and oral resonance, this is not included in the various presentations. The production is listed in the following form such as:

1. Vowel height: open, open-mid, closed-mid, and closed. The terms near-open and near-close are also used.
2. Frontness: back, central, and front are used.
3. Rounding: rounded and unrounded are used.

The vowels are discussed per their location on the vowel quadrilateral beginning with the /i/ and ending with the /ɑ/.

/i/—LOWER-CASE I

Parameters

The /i/ is a close, front, unrounded vowel.

Spellings

e as in we
ee as in geese
ea as in pea
ey as in key

Comments

1. The /i/ is a tense vowel and is often considered the most tense of all the vowels.
2. The duration of the /i/ vowel is long. The length varies depending on adjacent phonemes.

Monosyllabic Word Practice

1. Transcribe each of the following words into phonetics:

peek (peak)	beat (beet)	seed
keys	scene (seen)	deem
eat	fee	heap
leaves		

2. Count and record the number of phonemes per word.
3. Label each phoneme using the terms CV, VC, CVC, and so on.
4. Can the /i/ vowel appear in both open and closed syllables?

Reading Practice

1. Read each of the words written in phonetics aloud.
2. Write each of the words in orthography noting various spellings:

/ti/	/li/	/ik/
/nit/	/skim/	/sim/

/ɪ/—SMALL CAPITAL I

Parameters

The /ɪ/ is a near-close, front, unrounded vowel.

Spellings

i as in it
y as in hymn

Comments

1. The /ɪ/ appears only in close syllables. The use of the /ɪ/ with the understrike raising sign /ᵻ/, represents the /i/ sound in an unstressed syllable. The barred i /ɨ/ can also be used in similar situations. More information is presented on this in chapter 8.
2. The /ɪ/ appears frequently in GAP.
3. The /ɪ/ is difficult to pronounce for most ESL speakers. A common error is the substitution of the /i/ for the /ɪ/.
4. The /ɪ/ is a lax vowel.
5. The use of the iota /ι/ is no longer acceptable for the /ɪ/.

Monosyllabic Word Practice

1. Transcribe each of the following words into phonetics:

sit	limb	pick
fiz	give	kin
hip	bib	it
dim		

2. Count and record the number of phonemes per word.
3. Label each phoneme using the terms CV, VC, CVC, and so on.
4. Can the /ɪ/ vowel appear in both open and closed syllables?

Reading Practice

1. Read each of the words written in phonetics aloud.
2. Write each of the words in orthography noting various spellings:

/fig/   /milk/   /bin/
/lip/   /sik/   /if/

/e/—LOWER-CASE E

Parameters

The /e/ is a close-mid, front, unrounded vowel.

Spellings

a-e as in bake
ay as in pay
ai as in pain
ei as in eight
ey as in whey

Comments

1. The /e/ is a monothong. In American English some speakers pronounce the diphthong /eɪ/ in lieu of the monothong. See chapter 4 for more details.
2. The /e/ is a tense vowel.

Monosyllabic Word Practice

1. Transcribe each of the following words into phonetics:

make   bait   zane

maid (made)   gain   hey (hay)

Dave   face   pave

eight

2. Count and record the number of phonemes per word.
3. Label each phoneme using the terms CV, VC, CVC, and so on.
4. Can the /e/ vowel appear in both open and closed syllables?
5. Do you use the monothong or the diphthong in your speech?

Reading Practice

1. Read each of the words written in phonetics aloud.
2. Write each of the words in orthography noting various spellings:

/tem/	/kek/	/fe/
/ples/	/ek/	/ne/

/ɛ/—EPSILON

Parameters

The /ɛ/ is a open-mid, front, unrounded vowel.

Spellings

e as in bed
ea as in head

Comments

1. The /ɛ/ is a lax vowel.

Monosyllabic Word Practice

1. Transcribe each of the following words into phonetics:

fed	men	vet
said	bell	peck
hem	zest	net
sent		

2. Count and record the number of phonemes per word.
3. Label each phoneme using the terms CV, VC, CVC, and so on.
4. Can the /ɛ/ vowel appear in both open and closed syllables?

Reading Practice

1. Read each of the words written in phonetics aloud.
2. Write each of the words in orthography noting various spellings:

/lɛd/	/pɛn/	/bɛk/
/lɛt/	/sɛlf/	/ɛb/

/æ/—ASH

Parameters

The /æ/ is a near-open, front, unrounded vowel.

Spellings

a as in cat
a-e as in dance

Comments

1. The /æ/ is the most open, front vowel used in GAP. Some dialects use the open, front, round vowel /a/ in lieu of /æ/.
2. The /æ/ is a lax vowel.

Monosyllabic Word Practice

1. Transcribe each of the following words into phonetics:

sad	lance	man
back	van	ham
pass	tag	Zach
fad		

2. Count and record the number of phonemes per word.
3. Label each phoneme using the terms CV, VC, CVC, and so on.
4. Can the /æ/ vowel appear in both open and closed syllables?

Reading Practice

1. Read each of the words written in phonetics aloud.
2. Write each of the words in orthography noting various spellings:

/læf/	/fæt/	/sæm/
/mæk/	/æpt/	/æt/

/u/—LOWER-CASE U

Parameters

The /u/ is a close, back, rounded vowel.

Spellings

oo as in loom
o as in to
ew as in crew
ou as in soup
ui as in bruise
u-e as in rule

Comments

1. The /u/ is a tense vowel.
2. The /u/ is rarely used in GAP in the initial position of words. The /ju/ is used instead. See chapter 4 for more details.
3. In some words the /u/ and the /ʊ/ are used interchangeably.
4. The /ju/ and the /u/ are often used interchangeably in words like *new* [nu] or [nju] depending on the formality of the speaking situation (see chapter 10 for more details).

Monosyllabic Word Practice

1. Transcribe each of the following words into phonetics (do you pronounce the word using /u/ or /ju/?):

tube	zoom	do (dew or due)
goose	coup (coup)	fool
soon	tune	blew (blue)
loon		

2. Count and record the number of phonemes per word.
3. Label each phoneme using the terms CV, VC, CVC, and so on.
4. Can the /u/ vowel appear in both open and closed syllables?

Reading Practice

1. Read each of the words written in phonetics aloud.
2. Write each of the words in orthography noting various spellings:

| /but/ | /tu/ | /fud/ |
| /nuk/ | /sup/ | /skup/ |

/ʊ/—UPSILON

Parameters

The /ʊ/ is a near-close, back, rounded vowel.

Spellings

oo as in book
u as in push
ou as in could

Comments

1. There are few words in GAP that use the /ʊ/ phoneme.
2. The /ʊ/ is a lax vowel.
3. Many speakers use the /u/ and /ʊ/ interchangeably in conversational speech. Note the pronunciation of the words *coop, roof,* and *hoof.*
4. The omega /ɷ/ is no longer an acceptable alternate symbol for the /ʊ/.

Monosyllabic Word Practice

1. Transcribe each of the following words into phonetics:

bull	put	wolf
hood	soot	stood
full	could	

2. Count and record the number of phonemes per word.
3. Label each phoneme using the terms CV, VC, CVC, and so on.
4. Can the /ʊ/ vowel appear in both open and closed syllables?

Reading Practice

1. Read each of the words written in phonetics aloud.
2. Write each of the words in orthography noting various spellings:

/ʊps/	/hʊf/	/wʊf/
/kʊkt/	/bʊkt/	/lʊkt/

/o/—LOWER-CASE O

Parameters

The /o/ is a close-mid, back, rounded vowel.

Spellings

o as in no
ow as in tow
oe as in toe
oa as in coat
o-e as in rope

Comments

1. The /o/ is a monothong. Some speakers pronounce the diphthong /oʊ/ depending on context in lieu of the monothong. See chapter 4 for more details.
2. The /o/ is a tense vowel.

Monosyllabic Word Practice

1. Transcribe each of the following words into phonetics:

so (sew)	boast	goat
oak	hoe	foam
volt	nope	knoll
doze		

2. Count and record the number of phonemes per word.
3. Label each phoneme using the terms CV, VC, CVC, and so on.
4. Can the /o/ vowel appear in both open and closed syllables?
5. Do you use the monothong or the diphthong in your speech?

Reading Practice

1. Read each of the words written in phonetics aloud.
2. Write each of the words in orthography noting various spellings:

/kost/	/fold/	/stov/
/fo/	/ot/	/goz/

/ɔ/—OPEN O

Parameters

The /ɔ/ is a open-mid, back, rounded vowel.

Spellings

aw as in lawn
au as in auto
augh as in taught
ough as in ought

Comments

1. The use of the /ɔ/ is variable depending on dialect. Because the sound requires a distinct lip-rounded posture, the /ɑ/ is used as an alterative by some speakers whose speech is characterized by little or no lip rounding.
2. The /ɔ/ is a tense vowel.
3. The /ɔ/ is a long vowel.

Monosyllabic Word Practice

1. Transcribe each of the following words into phonetics:

paw	talk	caught
fawn	hawk	moss
log	ball	vaunt
soft		

2. Count and record the number of phonemes per word.
3. Label each phoneme using the terms CV, VC, CVC, and so on.
4. Can the /ɔ/ vowel appear in both open and closed syllables?
5. Do you use the /ɔ/ or the /ɑ/ in your speech?

Reading Practice

1. Read each of the words written in phonetics aloud.
2. Write each of the words in orthography noting various spellings:

/ɔ/	/bɔld/	/kɔ/
/lɔn/	/fɔl/	/tɔs/

/ʌ/—INVERTED V

Parameters

The /ʌ/ is a open-mid, back, unrounded vowel.

Spellings

u as in up
ou as in tough
o-e as in done

Comments

1. The /ʌ/ represents the neutral position of the articulators.
2. The /ʌ/ is a lax vowel.
3. The /ʌ/ has been considered a mid vowel in the past.

Monosyllabic Word Practice

1. Transcribe each of the following words into phonetics:

cup	tough	love
fun	hug	buck
sum (some)	bum	suds
hunt	of	

2. Count and record the number of phonemes per word.
3. Label each phoneme using the terms CV, VC, CVC, and so on.
4. Can the /ʌ/ vowel appear in both open and closed syllables?

Reading Practice

1. Read each of the words written in phonetics aloud.
2. Write each of the words in orthography noting various spellings:

/sʌn/	/hʌl/	/lʌg/
/tʌk/	/ʌp/	/mʌd/

/ɑ/—SCRIPT A

Parameters

The /ɑ/ is a open, back, unrounded vowel.

Spellings

al as in calm
o as in pop

Comments

1. The /ɑ/ is a tense vowel.

2. The /ɑ/ is a long vowel.
3. The /ɑ/ is infrequently found in final position of words.
4. The use of the /ɑ/ varies with dialect. For example the words *golf* and *fog* may be pronounced with either the /ɔ/ or the /ɑ/ vowels.

Monosyllabic Word Practice

1. Transcribe each of the following words into phonetics:

sod	dock	bomb
lot	ha	golf
fog	solve	odd
pot		

2. Count and record the number of phonemes per word.
3. Label each phoneme using the terms CV, VC, CVC, and so on.
4. Can the /ɑ/ vowel appear in both open and closed syllables?

Reading Practice

1. Read each of the words written in phonetics aloud.
2. Write each of the words in orthography noting various spellings:

/ɑ/	/stɑk/	/bɑks/
/ɑpt/	/tɑp/	/bɑ/

/ə/—SCHWA

Parameters

The /ə/ is a neutral, central, unrounded vowel.

Spellings

The schwa can be used to replace any vowel.

Comments

1. The schwa is used to replace any vowel in a unstressed syllable of a multisyllabic word. See chapter 8 for more details.
2. The schwa is a neutral vowel meaning that the height is equally between the open-mid and close-mid positions. It represents that entire vowel space.

Monosyllabic Word Practice

The schwa does not appear in monosyllabic words except in connected speech.

/ɜ/—REVERSED EPSILON

Parameters

The /ɜ/ open-mid, central, unrounded vowel.

Spellings

The /ɜ/ can be used to replace many different vowels.

Comments

1. The /ɜ/ sounds similar to the schwa but is used in stressed syllables.
2. The /ɜ/ is often combined with rhoticity in GAP in words such as *earn* [ɝn]. This is discussed in more detail in chapter 7.

Monosyllabic Word Practice

There are no monosyllabic words that use the /ɜ/ in GAP.

Acoustic Dimensions of Vowels

For purposes of production, vowels are generally described in terms of physical dimensions. It is important to stress; however, that describing vowels using physical dimensions only is both arbitrary and limited. Research in the area of acoustic phonetics provides significant information on the relationship between physical and acoustic properties of vowels. Although detailed information on acoustic phonetics is beyond the scope of this introductory text, the following information provides the beginning phonetician with some important background information on acoustic phonetics.

Sound is the result of changes in air pressure. Sound can be measured in cycles or by the time (**period**) it takes the air to move from and return to a resting position. The number of cycles completed in a given period of time is called the **frequency**.

Formants (vocal tract resonances) are strong concentrations of acoustic energy that can be measured in terms of vowel height, frontness, and roundness. Using conventional terminology the lowest formant (or fundamental frequency) is labeled **F1**, followed by **F2**, **F3**, and so on. Peterson and Barney (1952) determined average fundamental and formant frequencies for men, women and children. In a study by Hillenbrand, Getty, Clark, and Wheeler (1995), vowel reference points were modified reflecting current pronunciations and listener perceptions.

Cardinal Vowels

Cardinal vowels (see Fig. 3.2) are a series of eight absolute points described as reference points for vowel discussion. These exact vowels can not be measured in terms of acoustic values and were designed to be used as reference points. Cardinal Vowels 1 and 5 are defined in terms of tongue location and lip position. Vowels 2 through 4 are described as front vowels located in equal intervals below Cardinal 1. Vowels 6 through 8 are defined as back vowels located in equal intervals above Cardinal 5.

Although symbols that are the same as those used in GAP are used here, the cardinal vowels are not exactly the same as the actual GAP vowels. The principles of the IPA, however, do allow the symbols used for most of the GAP vowels to be the same as the nearby cardinal vowel. The use of the /a/ for the /æ/ is the one exception.[1]

---

[1]There is also a series of secondary cardinal vowels but these are beyond the scope of this introductory text.

1	i				u	8
	2	e			o	7
		3	ε		ɔ	6
			4	a	ɑ	5

FIG. 3.2. Primary cardinal vowel chart.

Although there are problems with the cardinal vowel system, it is important as a visual reference point for the understanding of vowels and vowel distance.

Vowel Spectrogram Tables

The spectrogram tablespresented here represent the static production of the vowel indicated as produced by a male talker. The **spectrograms** were produced using the Computerized Speech Laboratory (CSL). The vowels are measured using frequency as the vertical axis and time (measured in seconds) as the horizontal axis. As you view these spectrograms note the location of F1 and F2 and consider the following information:

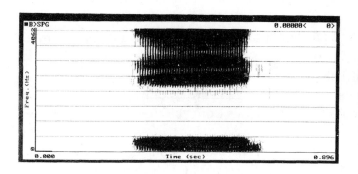

/i/

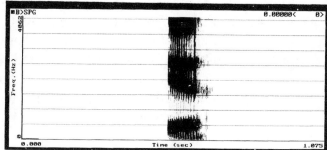

/ɪ/

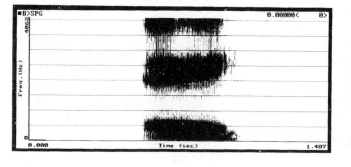

/e/

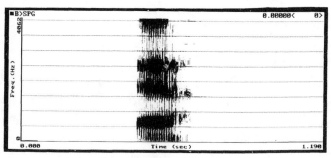

/ε/

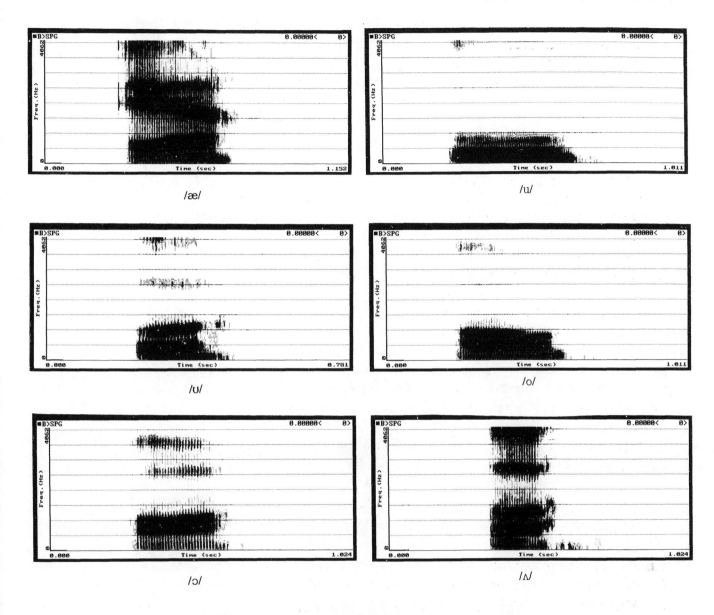

/æ/

/ʊ/

/ʊ/

/o/

/ɔ/

/ʌ/

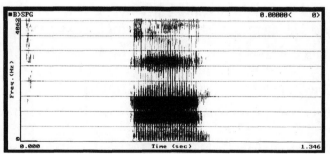

/ɑ/

1. Acoustically, vowel height is inversely proportional to the frequency of the first formant of the vowel.
2. Frontness refers to the location of the proportional difference between the frequency of the first and second formants.
3. The degree of lip rounding is complexly correlated to the acoustic correlates.
4. Vowels are affected by interaction of F1 and F2. The effect of F3 is less clear but seems to influence the accuracy of the perception of the vowel by the listener.

Review Questions

1. What are the three vowel dimensions?
2. What are the four vowel heights? What are the two supplemental positions?
3. What is the open vowel in GAP?
4. What are the closed vowels in GAP?
5. What is the near-open vowel in GAP? What is the near-close vowel?
6. What are the three degrees of frontness?
7. What are the back vowels in GAP?
8. What are the mid vowels in GAP?
9. What are the front vowels in GAP?
10. Give an example of a rounded vowel? Give an example of an unrounded vowel?
11. Why are vowels plotted in a quadrilateral space?
12. What do we mean by a tense vowel? What do we mean by a lax vowel?
13. List the vowels that have tense–lax pairs.
14. What is an open syllable? What is a closed syllable?
15. What vowels are always longer in duration in GAP?
16. Which vowel is the most tense of all vowels?
17. What are the two symbols used to represent the /i/ sound in an unstressed syllable?
18. What symbol is no longer an acceptable substitution for the /ɪ/ symbol according to the latest revision of the IPA?
19. What phonemes do ESL speakers often use instead of /ɪ/?
20. What are the two monothongs that are often pronounced as diphthongs?
21. What is the most open front, unrounded vowel in GAP?
22. What phoneme usually appears before /u/ in the initial position of words in GAP?
23. What vowel is often used interchangeably with the /u/ in conversational speech?
24. What symbol is no longer an acceptable substitution for the /ʊ/ symbol, according to the latest revision of the IPA?
25. What vowel is used by some speakers instead of /ɔ/? Why?
26. What do we mean when we say the /ʌ/ represents the neutral position of the articulators?
27. When is a schwa used?
28. What is combined with the reversed epsilon in GAP to provide r influence?
29. Define sound.
30. What is the period of a sound?
31. What is the frequency of a sound?
32. What is a formant?
33. Define F1 and F2.
34. What is a cardinal vowel?

35. Why are the cardinal vowels important?
36. How are vowels measured on a spectrogram?

Exercises

1. List the 13 vowels and describe each in terms of vowel height, frontness, and rounding.
2. List five monosyllabic words for each vowel and transcribe into phonetics for additional practice.
3. For purposes of review, do the following:
   - a. List all the close vowels used in GAP.
   - b. List all the front vowels used in GAP.
   - c. List all the back vowels used in GAP.
   - d. List all the rounded vowels used in GAP.
   - e. List all the unrounded vowels used in GAP.
   - f. List all the tense vowels used in GAP.
   - g. List all the lax vowels used in GAP.
   - h. List all the long vowels used in GAP.
   - i. List all the close-mid vowels used in GAP.
   - j. List all the open-mid vowels used in GAP.
   - k. List all the near-open vowels used in GAP.
   - l. List all the near-close vowels used in GAP.
   - m. List all the open vowels in GAP.
4. Transcribe the words *ooze, use* (both pronunciations), *coo*, and *cue, food,* and *feud*. Comments?
5. Transcribe the following tense–lax pairs into phonetics and label the phonological pattern. (These are common substitution patterns used by ESL speakers. Note how the wrong vowel pronunciation may change the meaning of the word.)

/i/ and /ɪ/

deal	dill
lead	lid
least	list
seat	sit
scene	sin
week	wick
sleep	slip
feet	fit
deep	dip
keep	kip

/e/ and /ɛ/

pain	pen
gate	get
weight (wait)	wet
laid	lead (led)
main	men
mace	mess
main (mane)	men
bake	beck
tamed	tend
saint	sent

/u/ and /ʊ/

kook	cook
stewed	stood
cooed	could
wooed	would (wood)
luke	look
pool	pull
fool	full
suit	soot

6. Transcribe the following contrasts into phonetics and label the phonological pattern.

/o/ and /ɔ/

oaf	off
coal	call

toll	tall
coast	cost
foul	fall
hole (whole)	hall
so (sew)	saw
low	law
hold	hauled
soul (sole)	Saul

/ʌ/ and /ʊ/

up	oop
son (sun)	soon
none (nun)	noon
done	dune
cup	coop
blood	blued
but	boot
bust	boost
muss	moose
does	dues

/ʌ/ and /ɑ/

cut	cat
duck	dock
some	psalm
hut	hot

bucks	box
nut	knot (not)
pup	pop
gut	got
done	don (Don)
come	calm

/æ/ and /ɛ/

had	head
man	men
add	Ed
sat	set
lad	led
knack	neck
dad	dead
mat	met

7. Label the vowel contrasts in Exercise 5 as to tense–tense, tense–lax, or lax–lax. For additional practice, write down five words for each other possible vowel contrast.

8. Using the /ɔ/ words in Exercise 5, write them in phonetics using the /ɑ/ vowel. Note the difference in pronunciation. Which pronunciation do you use? Try transcribing these words: *cot–caught, tot–taught,* and *not–naught.* Did the vowel differ?

NOTES

Chapter 4

Diphthongs

WHAT IS A DIPHTHONG?

A diphthong is a single sound produced when two vowels, one dominant in duration and stress and one reduced in duration and stress, are paired together in a sequence. Diphthongs are not included on the IPA charts because they are the result of the pairing two pure vowels. There are five diphthongs commonly used in GAP: /aɪ/, /aʊ/, /ɔɪ/, /eɪ/, and /oʊ/. In all cases, the first vowel is longer in duration and exhibits more stress. It is important to note that the close combination of the two vowels causes each of the vowels to lose its pure quality. The /ɪ/ in [aɪ] is quite different from the /ɪ/ in [ɪt]. Diphthongs can be found in both open and closed syllables. In phonological patterns, diphthongs are labeled using a single V symbol because the they act as one sound.

EXPLANATION OF DIPHTHONG PRESENTATION FORMAT

Because diphthongs are composed of vowels, it is best to describe them using the parameters of height, frontness, and rounding. The transition from the first to the second vowel is also included. Each diphthong is discussed in terms of parameters, a list of common orthographic interpretation (no attempt is made to include all possible spellings), a comments section, a list of monosyllabic words for practice, and a list of words written in phonetics for reading practice.

The parameters are listed using vowel height, frontness, and rounding of the first vowel and then the second vowel. Because all vowels require an open velopharyngeal port and oral resonance, this is also true of vowel combinations.

/aɪ/

Parameters

The /aɪ/ is a open, front, unrounded vowel moving to a near-close, front, unrounded vowel. The /a/ is longer in duration and forms the nucleus of the diphthong, while the /ɪ/ is shorter and unstressed.

Spellings

i as in time
y as in fly
ie as in tie
igh as in flight
i-e as in mice

Comments

1. The /aɪ/ varies in pronunciation depending on adjacent phonemes and dialectal variations.

Monosyllabic Word Practice

1. Transcribe each of the following words into phonetics:

ice	bye (buy or by)	pie
high (hi)	kind	five
dime	tine	lies
guise		

2. Count and record the number of phonemes per word.
3. Label each phoneme using the terms CV, VC, CVC, and so on.
4. Can the /aɪ/ diphthong appear in both open and closed syllables?

Reading Practice

1. Read each of the words written in phonetics aloud.
2. Write each of the words in orthography noting various spellings:

/laɪm/	/aɪd/	/aɪ/
/daɪv/	/haɪt/	/maɪnd/

/aʊ/

Parameters

The /aʊ/ is an open, front, unrounded vowel moving to a near-close, back, rounded vowel. The /a/ is longer in duration and forms the nucleus of the diphthong, while the /ʊ/ is shorter and unstressed.

Spellings

ow as in cow
ou as in loud

Comments

1. The pronunciation of the /aʊ/ will vary depending on adjacent phonemes and dialectal variations.
2. Note the w is silent in words such as *cow* [kaʊ].

Monosyllabic Word Practice

1. Transcribe each of the following words into phonetics:

town	cow	loud
pout	mouse	how
gown	found	bout

2. Count and record the number of phonemes per word.
3. Label each phoneme using the terms CV, VC, CVC, and so on.
4. Can the /aʊ/ diphthong appear in both open and closed syllables?

Reading Practice

1. Read each of the words written in phonetics aloud.
2. Write each of the words in orthography noting various spellings:

/aʊst/	/aʊt/	/baʊnd/
/maʊnd/	/daʊs/	/aʊns/

/ɔɪ/

Parameters

The /ɔɪ/ is an open-mid, back, rounded vowel moving to a near-close, front, unrounded vowel. The /ɔ/ is longer in duration and forms the nucleus of the diphthong, while the /ɪ/ is shorter and unstressed.

Spellings

oi as in boil
oy as in boy

Comments

1. The /ɔɪ/ diphthong appears infrequently in GAP.

Monosyllabic Word Practice

1. Transcribe each of the following words into phonetics:

point	hoist	void
loin	oil	coin
boils	moist	soy
cloy		

2. Count and record the number of phonemes per word.
3. Label each phoneme using the terms CV, VC, CVC, and so on.
4. Can the /ɔɪ/ diphthong appear in both open and closed syllables?

Reading Practice

1. Read each of the words written in phonetics aloud.
2. Write each of the words in orthography noting various spellings:

| /fɔɪst/ | /spɔɪl/ | /hɔɪ/ |
| /tɔɪ/ | /kɔɪl/ | /pɔɪ/ |

/eɪ/

Parameters

The /eɪ/ is a close-mid, front, unrounded vowel moving to a near-close, front, unrounded vowel. The /e/ is longer in duration and forms the nucleus on the diphthong, while the /ɪ/ is shorter and unstressed.

Spellings

ai as in brain
ay as in say
a-e as in rake

Comments

1. The /e/ and the /eɪ/ are used interchangeably by many GAP speakers. The representing /e/ the monothong and the /eɪ/ being the diphthong.

Monosyllabic Word Practice

1. Transcribe each of the following words into phonetics using both the /e/ vowel and the /eɪ/ diphthong:

bake	say	fade
knave	came	game
phase	laze	pace
lace		

2. Count and record the number of phonemes per word.
3. Label each phoneme using the terms CV, VC, CVC, and so on.
4. Can the /eɪ/ diphthong appear in both open and closed syllables?

Reading Practice

1. Read each of the words written in phonetics aloud.
2. Write each of the words in orthography noting various spellings:

/peɪs/	/neɪm/	/teɪst/
/veɪs/	/weɪd/	/heɪz/

/oʊ/

Parameters

The /oʊ/ is a close-mid, back, rounded vowel moving to a near-close, back, rounded vowel. The /o/ is longer in duration and forms the nucleus of the diphthong while the /ʊ/ is shorter and unstressed.

Spellings

o as in no
ow as in tow
oa as in groan
o-e as in rose

Comments

1. The /o/ and the /oʊ/ are used interchangeably by many GAP speakers. The representing /o/ the monothong and the /oʊ/ being the diphthong.

Monosyllabic Word Practice

1. Transcribe each of the following words into phonetics using both the /o/ vowel and the /oʊ/ diphthong:

toast	hoax	folk
coke	dough	moan
vogue	goad	pose

2. Count and record the number of phonemes per word.
3. Label each phoneme using the terms CV, VC, CVC, and so on.
4. Can the /oʊ/ diphthong appear in both open and closed syllables?

Reading Practice

1. Read each of the words written in phonetics aloud.
2. Write each of the words in orthography noting various spellings:

/oʊ/	/gloʊb/	/koʊm/
/boʊl/	/poʊl/	/doʊv/

ANOTHER DIPHTHONG?

Some authorities consider the /ju/ to be a sixth diphthong. This combination is frequently used in GAP. The following are three reasons to consider /ju/ a diphthong:

1. It involves two phonemes the /u/ vowel and the /j/, which historically was a version of the /i/ vowel.
2. The /ju/ appears frequently together yet the /j/ is not paired with other vowels in GAP.
3. The /ju/ does not fit into the consonant cluster category.

Following are two reasons to not consider /ju/ a diphthong.

1. It does not involve two vowels.
2. The nuclei of the diphthong appears at the end, while the shorter duration phoneme appears at the beginning.

The fact that the /ju/ appears frequently in GAP is the most important concept to grasp. The /ju/ can be considered either as a diphthong or a common pairing of an approximant and a vowel.

When used in the initial position of words, the /ju/ appears together in most situations such as in the word *use* [jus]. When appearing in the medial position of words, the /ju/ may be replaced by the /u/ such as in the word *new* [nju] or [nu]. The decision on which form is appropriate depends on the formality of the situation and the actual word. For example there is only one acceptable transcription of the word *few* [fju] (Ladefoged, 1993).

1. Transcribe each of the following words into phonetics using both the vowel /u/ and the diphthong /ju/ where appropriate:

use	fuse	you'll
you (ewe)	cue	Lou (lieu)
new	pew	

2. Count and record the number of phonemes per word.
3. Label each phoneme using the terms CV, VC, CVC, and so on.
4. Can the /ju/ appear in both open and closed syllables?

Reading Practice

1. Read each of the words written in phonetics aloud.
2. Write each of the words in orthography noting various spellings:

/hju/	/mjul/	/wju/
/kjub/	/njut/	/fjum/

Review Questions

1. How is a diphthong produced?
2. What are the five diphthongs in GAP?
3. In the diphthongs /aɪ/, /aʊ/, /ɔɪ/, /eɪ/, and /oʊ/ which part is longer in duration and forms the nucleus? Which part is shorter?
4. What influences the pronunciation of a particular diphthong?
5. List three facts that support /ju/ as a diphthong. List two facts that oppose it.

Exercises

1. Transcribe the following contrasts into phonetics and label the phonological pattern (remember the diphthong counts as one V, for example *night* [naɪt] = CVC):

/aɪ/ and /aʊ/

mice	mouse
by (bye or buy)	bow
high	how
file	fowl
find	found
type	taupe
bite	bout
dine	down
nine	noun
ply	plow

/ɔɪ/ and /aɪ/

toy	tie
loin	line
boy	buy
voice	vise
point	pint
oil	aisle
poise	pies
hoist	heist
toil	tile

/aʊ/ and /ɔɪ/

bow (bough)	boy
fowl (foul)	foil
cow	coy
pow	poi

2. Transcribe the following vowel–diphthong contrasts into phonetics and label the phonological pattern:

/i/ and /aɪ/

tea (tee)	tie
be (bee)	by (bye or buy)
Dee	die (dye)
feet	fight
he	hi
lee (Lee)	lie

me	my
niece	nice
pea	pie
see	sigh

/aɪ/ and /ɪ/

fine	fin
like	lick
type	tip
time (thyme)	Tim
night	nit (knit)
sign	sin
wife	whiff
bite	bit
hide	hid
light	lid

/aɪ/ and /ɑ/

light	lot
pipe	pop
type	top
like	lock
side	sod
night	not (knot)
wide	wad
time	Tom

| dine | Don (don) |
| high | ha |

/aʊ/ and /u/

down	dune
town	tune
gown	goon
cowl	cool
pout	pool
loud	leud
bow	boo
fowl	fool
spout	spool
bout	boot

/aʊ/ and /ɑ/

down	don (Don)
pout	pot
spout	spot
gout	got
lout	lot
taupe	top
naught	not (knot)
doubt	dot
cloud	clod
how	ha

/aʊ/ and /ʌ/

down	done
town	ton
gown	gun
cowl	cull
bout	but (butt)
pout	putt
gout	gut
mouse	muss
found	fund
noun	none (nun)

/ɔɪ/ and /ɔ/

coil	call
noise	gnaws
soy	saw
boil	ball
toi	tall
foil	fall

NOTES

Chapter 5

Consonants

As discussed in chapter 1, consonants are delineated by the IPA in terms of manner of articulation, place of articulation, and voicing. The five manners of articulation, the eight places of articulation and the concept of voicing used in GAP is described in detail. It is helpful to refer to Fig. 5.1 while reading the narrative explanations.

MANNER OF ARTICULATION

The five manners of articulation used in GAP are plosive, nasal, fricative, approximant, and lateral approximant. These represent the ways the air stream from the lungs or the sound stream from the larynx are modified by the articulators.

Plosive.   A plosive is a sound produced by the build up of air from the lungs behind a barrier. This is followed by a sudden release of the pressurized air. The two phases of a plosive production are called *implosion* and *explosion* (aspiration). Plosive sounds are sometimes referred to as stops. The plosive sounds in GAP are the cognates /p/ and /b/, /t/ and /d/, /k/, and /g/.

	Bilabial	Labiodental	Dental	Alveolar	Postalv.	Palatal	Velar	Glottal
Plosive	p,b			t,d			k,g	
Nasal	m			n			ŋ	
Fricative		f,v	θ,ð	s,z	ʃ,ʒ			h
Approximant				ɹ		j		
Lateral Approximant				l				

FIG. 5.1. General American Phonetics consonants chart. The vertical axis represents the manner of articulation, and the horizontal axis represents the place of articulation. Conventionally, the voiceless counterpart appears to the left of the voiced version.

Nasal. A nasal is a sound produced by emission of air through the nasal cavity. The velopharyngeal port is open during the production of a nasal sound. In GAP there are only three nasal sounds—/m/, /n/, and /ŋ/.

Fricative. A fricative is a sound characterized by the emission of a frictionlike noise created by the air stream escaping through a narrow orifice. The fricative sounds in GAP are the cognates /f/ and /v/, /θ/ and /ð/, /s/ and /z/, /ʃ/ and /ʒ/, and single consonant /h/.

Approximant. An approximant is a sound produced by the proximity of two articulators without turbulence. The approximant sounds in GAP are /ʍ/, /j/, and the combination approximant /w/.

Lateral Approximant. A lateral approximant possesses all the features of an approximant with the addition of the lateral flow of the air stream from the oral cavity. The only lateral approximant in GAP is the /l/.

PLACE OF ARTICULATION

The eight places of articulation in GAP are bilabial, labiodental, dental, alveolar, postalveolar, palatal, velar, and glottal. These are the places where the air stream from the lungs or the sound stream from the larynx is constricted by the articulators.

Bilabial. These sounds are produced the two lips. The bilabial sounds in GAP are the cognates /p/ and /b/, and the /m/ sound.

Labiodental. These sounds are produced by the placing of the four upper incisors in a resting posture on the lower lip. The labiodental sounds in GAP are /f/ and /v/.

Dental. These sounds are produced by the tongue protruding slightly through the upper and lower central incisors. The dental sounds in GAP are /θ/ and /ð/.

Alveolar. These sounds are produced by the tongue tip or blade gently approximating the alveolar ridge. The alveolar sounds in GAP are the cognates /t/ and /d/, and /s/ and /z/, and the sounds /n/, /ɹ/, and /l/.

Postalveolar. These sounds are produced by the tongue blade gently approximating the postalveolar ridge area. These sounds are also referred to by some authorities as palato-alveolar sounds. The postalveolar sounds in GAP are the cognates /ʃ/ and /ʒ/.

Palatal. This sound is produced by the tongue blade raised to meet the hard palate. The palatal sound in GAP is /j/.

Velar. These sounds are produced by the back of the tongue raising to meet the velum (soft palate). The velar sounds in GAP are the cognates /j/ and /g/ and the /ŋ/ sound.

Glottal. This sound is produced by the open position of the vocal folds that create the glottis. The /h/ is the only glottal sound in GAP.

VOICING

The aspects of **voicing** to consider are voiced consonants (those created by the vibration of the vocal folds during production) and voiceless or unvoiced consonants (those created by the absence of vibration of the vocal folds during production).

Figure 5.1 represents the 21 single consonants. GAP also uses four combination consonants:

/t ʃ/: voiceless alveolar–postalveolar fricative also called an affricate.

/dʒ/: voiced alveolar–postalveolar fricative also called an affricate.

/w/: voiced labial–velar approximant.

/ʍ/: voiceless labial–velar fricative.

There is one additional sound used in GAP called the /ʔ/ glottal sound. The glottal sound is a voiceless glottal plosive. It is used in American- English by some speakers to replace the /t/ in the medial position.

EXPLANATION OF CONSONANT PRESENTATION FORMAT

Each of the 21 single consonants, 4 combination consonants, and 1 other sound are discussed in detail. For each individual entry, the following information is provided: consonants presented in manner of articulation categories using cognates pairs when possible; the parameters, an explanation of the production, a description, a list of common orthographic interpretations (spelling), a comments section, and a list of monosyllabic words with the selected phoneme in the initial and final positions and a list of words written in phonetics for reading practice. (The monosyllabic word practice is designed to provide transcription practice, therefore, not all spelling or possible CV combinations are included.) The name of each phonetic symbol, according to Pullum and Ladusaw (1986), is also listed.

For purposes of clarity and consistency all parameters are discussed in terms of voicing, place of articulation, and then manner of articulation. The production is listed in a form such as:

1. Position of the vocal folds—open (voiceless sound) or vibrating (voiced sound).
2. Position of the velopharyngeal port—open (nasal sounds) or closed (oral sounds).
3. Position of the mandible—closed, slightly depressed (half way to the position of the /ɑ/), depressed (position of an /ɑ/).
4. Position of the lips—rounded, half rounded, spread.
5. Position of the tongue—neutral (resting on the floor of the mouth), or in a given location.

Due to the large amount of material covered in this chapter, it is divided into five sections. Each section has a set of review questions and exercises.

PLOSIVES

The first group of consonant phonemes presented are the plosives. This group includes the cognates /p/ and /b/, /t/ and /d/, /d/ and /g/. A **plosive** is a sound produced by the build up of air from the lungs behind a barrier. Plosives have two phases: an implosion stage and an explosion stage. During the implosion stage, air is trapped by a cavity created by two articulators. Following this phase there is a release of air called explosion. (Not all plosives have an explosive stage.)

/p/—LOWER-CASE P

Parameters

The /p/ is a voiceless, bilabial plosive.

Production

1. The vocal folds are open during both phases.
2. The velopharyngeal port is closed during both phases.
3. The mandible is closed during the implosion phase and slightly depressed during the explosion phase.
4. The lips are closed during the implosion phase and spread during the explosion phase.
5. The tongue is in a neutral position during both phases.

Description

The /p/ is produced when the air stream from the lungs is stopped by the lips building up intraoral pressure. When the pressure is released a puff of air is emitted.

Spellings

p as in pea, upon, and lip.
pp as in apple
mp as in lamp
pl as in please
spr as in spring
spl as in splash
sp as in lisp
mp as in limp
pt as in wept
lp as in help

Comments

1. The /p/ can be produced without tension using only the orbicularis oris muscle of the lips. When tension is applied, as in cases of emphasis or fluency problems, the buccinator and other facial expression muscles in the proximity of the lips become involved.

2. The /p/ can be produced with or without an explosion phase. If the explosion phase is present the symbol is written in narrow transcription as /p^h/. The superscript h (/^{h}/) is used to represent the presence of aspiration or the explosion of air.
3. The double p spelling is not pronounced and is retained from Old English where it was pronounced.
4. The /p/ is intrusive in selected words as in *something* [ˈsʌmp ˈθɪŋ]. It is used for ease of pronunciation.

Monosyllabic Word Practice

1. Transcribe each of the following words into phonetics:

pea	Paul (pall)	pause
pay	pop	poise
pep	putt	pow
pew	camp	splice
pope	pin	stop
pull	scalp	pat
wept	spy	

2. Count and record the number of phonemes per word.
3. Label each phoneme using the terms CV, VC, CVC, and so on.
4. Which of the 11 vowels and 3 major diphthongs are not represented in the word practice?
5. Can you think of a monosyllabic word that has /p/ in the initial or final position and contains the vowels or diphthongs not represented?

Reading Practice

1. Read each of the words written in phonetics aloud.
2. Write each of the words in orthography noting various spellings:

/plɔɪ/	/pul/	/pel/
/pil/	/pækt/	/pʌb/

/b/—LOWER-CASE B

Parameters

The /b/ is a voiced, bilabial plosive.

Production

1. The vocal folds are vibrating during both phases.

2. The velopharyngeal port is closed during both phases.
3. The mandible is closed during the implosion phase and slightly depressed during the explosion phase.
4. The lips are closed during the implosion phase and spread during the explosion phase.
5. The tongue is in a neutral position during both phases.

Description

The /b/ is produced when the voiced air stream from the larynx is stopped by the lips building up intraoral pressure. When the pressure is released, a puff of voiced air is emitted.

Spellings

b as in bee, robin, and cob
bb as in ribbon
mb as in comb
bl as in blue (blew)

Comments

1. The /b/ can be produced without tension using only the orbicularis oris muscle of the lips. When tension is applied, as in cases of emphasis or fluency problems, the buccinator and other facial expression muscles in the proximity of the lips become involved.
2. The double b spelling is not pronounced and is retained from the Old English where it was pronounced.

Monosyllabic Word Practice

1. Transcribe each of the following words into phonetics:

be (bee)	bug	bin
bay	bed	black
boat	bop	book
bat	boo	bought
climb	Ben (been)	bow
boy		

2. Count and record the number of phonemes per word.
3. Label each phoneme using the terms CV, VC, CVC, and so on.
4. Which of the 11 vowels and 3 major diphthongs are not represented in the word practice?
5. Can you think of a monosyllabic word that has /b/ in the initial or final position and contains the vowels or diphthongs not represented?

Reading Practice

1. Read each of the words written in phonetics aloud.
2. Write each of the words in orthography noting various spellings:

/bæn/	/bist/	/bɛg/
/bʌs/	/bum/	/bes/

/t/—LOWER-CASE T

Parameters

The /t/ is a voiceless, alveolar plosive.

Production

1. The vocal folds are open during both phases.
2. The velopharyngeal port is closed during both phases.
3. The mandible is slightly depressed during the implosion phase and depressed during the explosion phase.
4. The lips are spread during both phases.
5. The tongue tip is elevated to the alveolar ridge and the side of the tongue touches the inside of the upper teeth during implosion. During explosion the tongue tip lowers to the area behind the lower central incisors.

Description

The /t/ is produced when the air stream from the lungs is stopped by the tip of the tongue resting on the alveolar ridge building up intraoral pressure in the small cavity created. When the pressure is released, a puff of air is emitted.

Spellings

t as in tea, guitar, at
th as in Thomas
bt as in debt

Comments

1. The /t/ can also be produced by placing the tongue on either the upper or lower central incisors. The is called a dental / t̪ / written in narrow transcription with the subscript bridge /t̪/.
2. The /t/ can be produced with or without an explosion phase. In narrow transcription the /tʰ/ is used to represent the presence of aspiration or the explosion of air.
3. In American-English the medial /t/ is not always pronounced as a /t/. It is pronounced as a /d/ or a partially voiced /t/ (written in narrow transcription with the subscript wedge /t̬/ in words like *butter*

['bʌd ə'] or ['buṯ ə]. It can be pronounced as a glottal /ʔ/ in words like *mitten* ['mɪʔ ən] where the /ʔ/ is followed by certain phonemes. In British-English the medial /t/ is still produced in most words.

4. The /t/ phoneme is also used in GAP to denote past tense. Because the /t/ is a voiceless phoneme, it is used to form the past tense of words ending in a voiceless phoneme such as *cooked* [kʊkt].

Monosyllabic Word Practice

1. Transcribe each of the following words into phonetics:

team	tool	took
tin	take	tent
tan	taught	toe
tot	tub	doubt
cat	Tim	toil

thyme (time)

2. Count and record the number of phonemes per word.
3. Label each phoneme using the terms CV, VC, CVC, and so on.
4. Which of the 11 vowels and 3 major diphthongs are not represented in the word practice?
5. Can you think of a monosyllabic word that has the /t/ in the initial or final position and contains the vowels or diphthongs not represented?

Reading Practice

1. Read each of the words written in phonetics aloud.
2. Write each of the words in orthography noting various spellings:

/tɪl/	/taɪt/	/tæks/
/tɛst/	/tʌn/	
/tod/		

/d/—LOWER-CASE D

Parameters

The /d/ is a voiced, alveolar plosive.

Production

1. The vocal folds are vibrating during both phases.

2. The velopharyngeal port is closed during both phases.
3. The mandible is slightly depressed during the implosion phase and depressed during the explosion phase.
4. The lips are spread during both phases.
5. The tongue tip is elevated to the alveolar ridge and the sides of tongue touch the inside of the upper teeth during implosion. During explosion, the tongue tip is lowers to the area behind the lower central incisors.

Description

The /d/ is produced when the voiced air stream from the larynx is stopped by the tip of the tongue resting on the alveolar ridge building up intraoral pressure in this small cavity. When the pressure is released, a puff of voiced air is emitted.

Spellings

d as in den, meadow, and bid
ld as in could
dd as in ladder
ed as in molded

Comments

1. The /d/ can also be produced by placing the tongue on either the upper or lower central incisors. This is called a dental /d̪/ written in narrow transcription with /d̪/ the subscript bridge.
2. The /d/ symbol is used in GAP to denote past tense. Because the /d/ is a voiced phoneme, it is used to form the past tense of words ending in a voiced phoneme such as *clubbed* [klʌbd]. In some cases a /əd/ is also used to form the past tense.

Monosyllabic Word Practice

1. Transcribe each of the following words into phonetics:

deed	dupe	did
day	dead	dad
Don (don)	dole	done
die (dye)	dowel	would (wood)
dawn	dot	

2. Count and record the number of phonemes per word.
3. Label each phoneme using the terms CV, VC, CVC, and so on.
4. Which of the 11 vowels and 3 major diphthongs are not represented in the word practice?
5. Can you think of a monosyllabic word that has /d/ in the initial or final position and contains the vowels or diphthongs not represented?

Reading Practice

1. Read each of the words written in phonetics aloud.
2. Write each of the words in orthography noting various spellings:

/dʌb/   /dɪp/   /dɛlv/
/dæns/   /dun/   /dʌg/

/k/—LOWER-CASE K

Parameters

The /k/ is a voiceless, velar plosive.

Production

1. The vocal folds are open during both phases.
2. The velopharyngeal port is closed during both phases
3. The mandible is depressed during both phases.
4. The lips are open and half rounded.
5. The back of the tongue is elevated and retracted at the point of junction between the velum and the palatine bones. The sides of the tongue are touching the inside of the molars.

Description

The /k/ is produced when the air stream from the lungs is stopped by the back of tongue, which is blocking the air stream near the velum. There is a build up of pressure in the pharyngeal area, followed by a release of air.

Spellings

k as in key, akin, cook
sc as in scare
sk as in skip
qu as in queen
nk as in trunk
cc as in accord
c as in tic
ck as in black
cl as in clerk

Comments

1. The /k/ can be produced with or without an explosion phase. In narrow transcription the /kʰ/ is used to represent the presence of aspiration or the explosion of air.
2. The /k/ spelling was not introduced until Middle English. Prior to this, the c was used. The use of both c and k orthographic symbols to represent the /k/ phoneme comes from the inclusion of loanwords.

3. The /k/ is intruded in selected words such as *length* [lɛŋkθ].
4. The nk spelling is actually pronounced and transcribed as /ŋk/ as in the word *sink* [sɪŋk].
5. Remember, many words in the English language are spelled with the letter c but the correct phoneme is /k/.

Monosyllabic Word Practice

1. Transcribe each of the following words into phonetics:

key	Kim	cape
kept	cap	kook
cook	coat	cause
cot	wake	bunk
slack	clap	bic
skate	cow	quilt
scat	cut	kite
coy		

2. Count and record the number of phonemes per word.
3. Label each phoneme using the terms CV, VC, CVC, and so on.
4. Which of the 11 vowels and 3 major diphthongs are not represented in the word practice?
5. Can you think of a monosyllabic word that has /k/ in the initial or final position and contains the vowels or diphthongs not represented?

Reading Practice

1. Read each of the words written in phonetics aloud.
2. Write each of the words in orthography noting various spellings:

/kon/	/ken/	/kɑn/
/kɪs/	/kʌb/	/kol/

/g/—LOWER-CASE G

Parameters

The /g/ is a voiced, velar plosive.

Production

1. The vocal folds are vibrating during both phases.

2. The velopharyngeal port is closed during both phases.
3. The mandible is depressed during both phases.
4. The lips are open and half rounded.
5. The back of the tongue is elevated and retracted at the point of junction between the velum and the palatine bones. The sides of the tongue are touching the inside of the molars.

Description

The /g/ is produced when the voiced air stream from the larynx is stopped by the back of the tongue, which is blocking the air stream near the velum. There is a build up of pressure in the pharyngeal area, followed by a release of voiced air.

Spellings

g as in go, tiger, and bag
gg as in trigger
gh as in ghost
gu as in guess
x as in exist
gl as in glue

Comments

1. The ng spelling as in *bang* is not the /g/ but the /ŋ/ phoneme.
2. The /g/ sound has a long history in our language. See the appendices for more detailed information.

Monosyllabic Word Practice

1. Transcribe each of the following words into phonetics:

glee	Whig (wig)	gate
get	gap	goon
good	go	gaunt
gun	guide	big
gout	ghoul	vague
grey	gob	

2. Count and record the number of phonemes per word.
3. Label each phoneme using the terms CV, VC, CVC, and so on.
4. Which of the 11 vowels and 3 major diphthongs are not represented in the word practice?
5. Can you think of a monosyllabic word that has /g/ in the initial or final position and contains the vowels or diphthongs not represented?

Reading Practice

1. Read each of the words written in phonetics aloud.
2. Write each of the words in orthography noting various spellings:

/gɪld/   /gɛs/   /gez/

/gʌl/   /gɪg/   /gost/

Review Questions

1. What are the five manners of articulation in GAP?
2. What are the eight places of articulation in GAP?
3. When a consonant phoneme is voiced, where does the air stream come from? When a consonant is voiceless, where does the air stream come from?
4. What are the four combination consonants? Why are they called combinations?
5. What are the two plosive phases called?
6. Are the two plosive phases always present?
7. What lip muscle is used when the /p/ and /b/ are produced without tension?
8. When is tension present in the production of the /p/ and /b/?
9. Aspiration is associated with what phase of the plosive?
10. What is meant by an intrusive /p/?
11. How is a dental /t/ or /d/ produced? How are they noted in narrow transcription?
12. In GAP, what three phoneme or sounds replace the medial /t/ in pronunciation?
13. Are the /t/ and /d/ used as past tense markers?
14. What letter is commonly used in orthography to represent the /k/ phoneme?
15. Is there a /g/ in the word *sing*? What is the final phoneme?

Exercises

1. List the 21 single consonants and describe each in terms of voicing, place, and manner.
2. List the four combination consonants and describe each in terms of voicing, place, and manner.
3. Transcribe the following cognates into phonetics and label the phonological pattern:

/p/ and /b/

pea	bee (be)
pay	bay
pop	bop
pull	bull
putt	but
tap	tab

robe	rope
poise	boys
pill	bill

/t/ and /d/

team	deem
tin	din
tan	Dan
ton	done
tune	dune
tub	dub
thyme (time)	dime
tent	dent
toe	doe
mat	mad

/k/ and /g/

could	good
tack	tag
key	G
cut	gut
cape	tape
coat	goat
cap	gap
cool	ghoul
came	game
wick	wig

4. Transcribe the following voiceless contrasts into phonetics and label the phonological pattern:

/p/ and /t/

rope	wrote (rote)
pie	tie
pin	tin
pop	top
pea	tea
poise	toys
pop	pot
pan	tan
cap	cat
pub	tub

/p/ and /k/

pan	can
peep	keep
pot	cot
putt	cut
pause	cause
pow	cow
pain	cane
pop	cop
pat	cat
pea	key

/t/ and /k/

tee (tea)	key
tan	can
tot	cot
top	cop
tub	cub
tin	kin
tap	cap
putt	puck
Tim	Kim
toil	coil

5. Transcribe the following voiced contrasts into phonetics and label the phonological pattern:

/b/ and /d/

bay	day
Ben	den
bug	Doug (dug)
bed	dead
bin	din
bead	deed
bye (buy or by)	die (dye)
bowl	dole
bid	did
ban	Dan

/b/ and /g/

bib	big
bowl	goal
bow	go
big	gig
bet	get
bun	gun
bay	gay
bye (buy or by)	guy
blue	glue
boat	goat

/d/ and /g/

day	gay
die	guy
dole	goal
dawn	gone
doe	go
done	gun
debt	get
bid	big
date	gate
daunt	gaunt

NASALS

The next group of sounds presented is the nasals. This group includes the /m/, /m/, and /ŋ/. A nasal sound is produced by emission of air through the nasal cavity with an open velopharyngeal port.

/m/—LOWER-CASE M

Parameters

The /m/ is a voiced, bilabial nasal.

Production

1. The vocal folds are vibrating.
2. The velopharyngeal port is open.
3. The mandible is closed.
4. The lips are closed.
5. The tongue is in a neutral position.

Description

The /m/ is produced when the voiced air stream from the larynx is stopped by the lips and redirected through the nasal cavity. The sound is released through the nasal cavity.

Spellings

m as in me, family, and am
mm as in summer
mb as in climb
mn as in hymn
lm as in realm
gm as in diaphragm
mp as in lamp

Comments

1. The /m/ is the easiest to produce of all the consonant phonemes. For this reason, it is one of the first sounds produced by infants.
2. The /m/ is produced using the same place of articulation as the /b/. The difference between the two phonemes is the nasal release of the voiced air stream when the /m/ is produced. If a person's voice is denasal (the nasal cavity is blocked) in quality, the /b/ may be substituted for the /m/ in conversational speech.
3. Some authorities refer to the /m/ as a stop with nasal resonance.

Monosyllabic Word Practice

1. Transcribe each of the following words into phonetics:

me	moot	lamb
mix	moat	vamp
may	meet (meat)	mat
mine	mount	lymph
Mike	palm	tomb

2. Count and record the number of phonemes per word.
3. Label each phoneme using the terms CV, VC, CVC, and so on.
4. Which of the 11 vowels and 3 major diphthongs are not represented in the word practice?
5. Can you think of a monosyllabic word that has /m/ in the initial or final position and contains the vowels or diphthongs not represented?

Reading Practice

1. Read each of the words written in phonetics aloud.
2. Write each of the words in orthography noting various spellings:

| /mez/ | /mɪl/ | /mæp/ |
| /mɛs/ | /mʌl/ | /maɪt/ |

/n/—LOWER-CASE N

Parameters

The /n/ is a voiced, alveolar nasal.

Production

1. The vocal folds are vibrating.
2. The velopharyngeal port is open.
3. The mandible is slightly depressed.
4. The lips are spread.
5. The tongue tip is elevated to the alveolar ridge and the sides of the tongue touch the inside of the upper teeth.

Description

The /n/ is produced when the voiced air stream from the larynx is stopped by the tip of the tongue resting on the alveolar ridge. The voiced air stream is then released through the nasal cavity.

Spellings

n as in need, tiny, and can.
nn as in pinning
kn as in knee
gn as in gnome
pn as in pneumonia
mn as in mnemonic

Comments

1. The first phoneme in the /n/ blends (gn, kn, pn, and mn) became silent during Middle English.
2. The /n/ is produced using the same place of articulation as the /d/. The difference between the two phonemes is the nasal release of the voiced air stream when the /n/ is produced. If a person's voice is denasal in quality, the /d/ may be substituted for the /n/ in conversational speech.
3. Note the varied meaning of the words with the kn versus n spellings, for example *knight* and *night*.

Monosyllabic Word Practice

1. Transcribe each of the following words into phonetics:

knee	need (knead)	nit (knit)
naked	neck	nook
new (knew)	no (know)	nut
naught	not (knot)	knife
sign	now	on
nap (knap)	noise	gnaw

Nick (nick)

2. Count and record the number of phonemes per word.
3. Label each phoneme using the terms CV, VC, CVC, and so on.
4. Which of the 11 vowels and 3 major diphthongs are not represented in the word practice?
5. Can you think of a monosyllabic word that has /n/ in the initial or final position and contains the vowels or diphthongs not represented?

Reading Practice

1. Read each of the words written in phonetics aloud.
2. Write each of the words in orthography noting various spellings:

/nun/   /nɑd/
/nɪp/   /naɪn/
/nɛt/   /nɪks/

/ŋ/—ENG

Parameters

The /ŋ/ is a voiced, velar nasal.

Production

1. The vocal folds are vibrating.
2. The velopharyngeal port is open.
3. The mandible is depressed.
4. The lips are open and half rounded.
5. The back of the tongue is elevated and retracted. It is placed in contact with the roof of the mouth at the point of junction between the velum and the palatine bones. The sides of the tongue are touching the inside of the molars.

Description

The /ŋ/ is produced when the voiced air stream from the larynx is stopped by the back of the tongue which is blocking the air stream near the velum. The voiced air stream is redirected through the nasal cavity.

Spellings

ng as in ring
nk as in ink
nc as in uncle
ng as in long or tongue
nx as in jinx

Comments

1. Historically, the /ŋ/ was an allophonic variation of the /n/. This may account for the variety of spellings used to represent the /n/.
2. The /ŋ/ is produced using the same place of articulation as the /g/. The difference between the two phonemes is the nasal release of the voiced air stream when the /ŋ/ is produced. If a person's voice is denasal (the nasal cavity is blocked) in quality, the /g/ may be substituted for the /ŋ/ in conversational speech.
3. The /ŋ/ phoneme appears in the medial and final positions of words in GAP.
4. Due to phonological rules, the /ŋ/ can only be combined with certain vowels in GAP. See chapter 7 for more details.
5. The nk spelling is pronounced /ŋk/ in GAP in words such as *sink* [sɪŋk].
6. The ng spelling is often pronounced as /ŋg/ as in *long* [lɔŋg] by speakers using an eastern dialect.

Monosyllabic Word Practice

1. Transcribe each of the following words into phonetics.

sing   long   lung

rank   ping   tang

tongue   lynx

2. Count and record the number of phonemes per word.
3. Label each phoneme using the terms CV, VC, CVC, and so on.
4. Which of the 11 vowels and 3 major diphthongs are not represented in the word practice?
5. Can you think of a monosyllabic word that has /ŋ/ in the initial or final position and contains the vowels or diphthongs not represented?

Reading Practice

1. Read each of the words written in phonetics aloud.
2. Write each of the words in orthography noting various spellings:

/wɪŋ/   /bæŋ/
/flɪŋ/   /sʊŋ/
/dɑŋ/   /pɔŋ/

Review Questions

1. During the production of nasal phonemes, how is the air stream emitted?
2. What happens anatomically to produce the nasal phonemes?
3. What nasal phoneme is produced early in speech development?
4. When the nasal cavity is blocked, which phoneme does the /m/ phoneme resemble— /n/ or /ŋ/?
5. How are the gn, kn, pn, and mn blends pronounced?
6. What is the name of the /ŋ/ symbol?
7. In what positions of words does the /ŋ/ appear?
8. In the nk spelling, as in the word *drink*, how is the nk transcribed?

Exercises

1. Transcribe the following contrasts into phonetics and label the phonological pattern (note the presence of the silent g and k):

/n/ and /m/

nine	mine
knee	me
nay (neigh)	may
neat	meat (meet)
gnat	mat
knob	mob
run	rum
knap (nap)	map
no	mow
net	met

/n/ and /ŋ/

sin	sing
ton	tongue
ran	rang
lawn	long
win	wing
sun	sung
thin	thing
kin	king
Len	length
win	wing

/m/ and /ŋ/

tam	tang
ram	rang
whim	wing
Kim	king
sum	sung
ham	hang
rim	wring (ring)
slam	slang
pom	pong
brim	bring

FRICATIVES

The fricative phonemes include the cognates /f/ and /v/, /θ/ and /ð/, /s/ and /z/, /ʃ/ and /ʒ/, and the single consonant /h/. A fricative sound is characterized by emission of a frictionlike noise created by the air stream escaping a narrow orifice.

/f/—LOWER-CASE F

Parameters

The /f/ is a voiceless, labiodental fricative.

Production

1. The vocal folds are open.
2. The velopharyngeal port is closed.
3. The mandible is slightly depressed.
4. The lips spread with the upper incisors resting gently on the lower lip.
5. The tongue is in the neutral position.

Description

The /f/ is produced when the air stream from the lungs is modified by the narrow orifice created by the closure of the upper incisors resting gently on the lower lip.

Spellings

f as in fin, before, and if
ff as in coffee
gh as in laugh
ph as in phone
lf as in calf
fl as in fly

Comments

1. The /f/ is a result of low frequency vibrations from the larynx combined with high frequency friction noises at the orifice.

Monosyllabic Word Practice

1. Transcribe each of the following words into phonetics:

puff	feet	fin
faint	fest	fast
foot	float	fought
staff	fight	cough
phone	foul	half
Fred	goof	foil

2. Count and record the number of phonemes per word.
3. Label each phoneme using the terms CV, VC, CVC, and so on.
4. Which of the 11 vowels and 3 major diphthongs are not represented in the word practice?
5. Can you think of a monosyllabic word that has /f/ in the initial or final position and contains the vowels or diphthongs not represented?

Reading Practice

1. Read each of the words written in phonetics aloud.
2. Write each of the words in orthography noting various spellings:

/ɔf/	/fɑks/	/fid/
/feɪl/	/fæks/	/fɪlm/

/v/—LOWER-CASE V

Parameters

The /v/ is a voiced, labiodental fricative.

Production

1. The vocal folds are vibrating.
2. The velopharyngeal port is closed.
3. The mandible is slightly depressed.
4. The lips spread with the upper incisors resting gently on the lower lip.
5. The tongue is in the neutral position.

Description

The /v/ is produced when the voiced air stream from the larynx is modified by the narrow orifice created by the closure of the upper incisors resting gently on the lower lip.

Spellings

v as in van, river, and have
vv as in savvy
lv as in salve

Comments

1. The /v/ is a result of low frequency vibrations from the larynx combined with high frequency friction noises at the orifice.
2. The /v/ is an infrequently used phoneme in the GAP. It was originally adopted into the language during Middle English for use in French loanwords.
3. In the history of the language, /v/ was used instead of the /w/ as in the Old Norse [vif] for *wife*.

Monosyllabic Word Practice

1. Transcribe each of the following words into phonetics:

vie	vote	vow
vat	vein (vain or vane)	vine
delve	glove	gave
vault	voice	live
v	view	

2. Count and record the number of phonemes per word.
3. Label each phoneme using the terms CV, VC, CVC, and so on.
4. Which of the 11 vowels and 3 major diphthongs are not represented in the word practice?
5. Can you think of a monosyllabic word that has /v/ in the initial or final position and contains the vowels or diphthongs not represented?

Reading Practice

1. Read each of the words written in phonetics aloud.
2. Write each of the words in orthography noting various spellings:

/hæv/	/klov/	/vɪm/
/vɛst/	/vog/	/vɛnd/

/θ/—THETA

Parameters

The /θ/ is a voiceless, dental fricative.

Production

1. The vocal folds are open.
2. The velopharyngeal port is closed.
3. The mandible is slightly depressed.
4. The lips are spread.
5. The tongue is elevated. The tongue protrudes slightly between the upper and lower central incisors.

Description

The /θ/ is produced when the air stream from the lungs is modified by the a wide, shallow orifice created by the protrusion of the tongue between the upper and lower incisors.

Spellings

th as in thank, nothing, and oath.

Comments

1. The th is the only spelling of the /θ/.
2. The voiceless th was originally written as either the /þ/ thorn or the /ð/ eth. As time progressed, the /ð/ eth began to be used between two vowels and was voiced. In Early Modern English, the /θ/ theta was introduced and was gradually replaced with the th spelling.
3. The /θ/ is one of the weakest sounds acoustically.

4. Very few languages use the /θ/ sound; thus, ESL students find this phoneme difficult to pronounce and often substitute another phoneme.
5. Speakers using African-American English (AAE) often substitute the /f/ for the /θ/ phoneme.

Monosyllabic Word Practice

1. Transcribe each of the following words into phonetics:

theme	thin	theft
thud	thru (threw)	bath
cloth	mouth	both
thigh	faith	moth

2. Count and record the number of phonemes per word.
3. Label each phoneme using the terms CV, VC, CVC, and so on.
4. Which of the 11 vowels and 3 major diphthongs are not represented in the word practice?
5. Can you think of a monosyllabic word that has /θ/ in the initial or final position and contains the vowels or diphthongs not represented?

Reading Practice

1. Read each of the words written in phonetics aloud.
2. Write each of the words in orthography noting various spellings:

/θɔ/	/θɪk/	/θɔt/
/θʌg/	/θɪŋ/	/θɑŋ/

/ð/—ETH

Parameters

The /ð/ is a voiced, dental fricative.

Production

1. The vocal folds are vibrating.
2. The velopharyngeal port is closed.
3. The mandible is slightly depressed.
4. The lips are spread.
5. The tongue is elevated. The tongue protrudes slightly between the upper and lower central incisors.

Description

The /ð/ is produced when the voiced air stream from the larynx is modified by the a wide, shallow orifice created by the protrusion of the tongue between the upper and lower central incisors.

Spellings

th as in the, bother, and bathe

Comments

1. The th is the only spelling of the /ð/.
2. The /ð/ has a long history. The symbol itself originated from the Old English use of the d (from the Roman alphabet) with a horizontal line in the stem section. It was used with the th sound appeared before the r . In the 15th century, the scribes began to use the y to replace the eth. This introduced words like *Ye* into the language. The /ð/ became voiced during the modern period and is now represented by the th spelling.
3. The /ð/ is difficult for ESL speakers because very few languages use the sound.
4. The /ð/ is one of the last sounds mastered by children.

Monosyllabic Word Practice

1. Transcribe each of the following words into phonetics:

these	this	bathe
clothe	soothe	those
thus	they	than
thou	then	scythe

2. Count and record the number of phonemes per word.
3. Label each phoneme using the terms CV, VC, CVC, and so on.
4. Which of the 11 vowels and 3 major diphthongs are not represented in the word practice?
5. Can you think of a monosyllabic word that has /ð/ in the initial or final position and contains the vowels or diphthongs not represented?

Reading Practice

1. Read each of the words written in phonetics aloud.
2. Write each of the words in orthography noting various spellings:

/ðɛns/	/ðæt/	/ðɛm/
/ðaɪn/	/taɪð/	/sið/

/s/—LOWER-CASE S

Parameters

The /s/ is a voiceless, alveolar fricative.

Production

1. The vocal folds are open.
2. The velopharyngeal port is closed.
3. The mandible is slightly depressed.
4. The lips are spread.
5. The tongue is elevated and grooved. The tongue tip touches the alveolar ridge between the upper central incisors. The sides of the tongue touch the inside of the upper teeth.

Description

The /s/ is produced when the air stream from the lungs is modified by the a narrow, shallow orifice created by the slightly downward deflect of a grooved tongue. The air stream creates a frictionlike sound as it passes the edges of the teeth.

Spellings

s as in sun, basin, and gas
sp as in spy
ss as in kiss
st as in sting
c as in city
str as in string
ps as in psalm
sk as in ski
z as in waltz
sn as in snow
sc as in scare
x as in fox

Comments

1. The second acceptable acoustic variation of the alveolar /s/ is called the dental /s/. In the production of this phoneme, the tongue tip is raised toward the alveolar ridge, deflecting the air stream upward.
2. The /s/ spelling is often pronounced as a /z/.
3. The /s/ is the most frequent consonant sound in GAP. The frequency is due in part to the use of the /s/ to form the regular plural in words ending with voiceless consonants. The exception to this rule are words ending with /s/ that form their plural using the /əz/.
4. The /s/ is one of the most frequently misarticulated phonemes affected by dentition, hearing loss, and complexity of production.

Monosyllabic Word Practice

1. Transcribe each of the following words into phonetics:

see	sin	sane
sex	sax (sacks)	sock (sox)
miss	sue (Sue)	stood
sauce	pops	soil
sky	street	souse
snow	stuck	psalm

2. Count and record the number of phonemes per word.
3. Label each phoneme using the terms CV, VC, CVC, and so on.
4. Which of the 11 vowels and 3 major diphthongs are not represented in the word practice?
5. Can you think of a monosyllabic word that has /s/ in the initial or final position and contains the vowels or diphthongs not represented?

Reading Practice

1. Read each of the words written in phonetics aloud.
2. Write each of the words in orthography noting various spellings:

/sænd/	/sɪt/	/sut/
/sol/	/sɛnd/	/sem/

/z/—LOWER-CASE Z

Parameters

The /z/ is a voiced, alveolar fricative.

Production

1. The vocal folds are vibrating.
2. The velopharyngeal port is closed.
3. The mandible is slightly depressed.
4. The lips are spread.
5. The tongue is elevated and grooved. The tongue tip touches the alveolar ridge between the upper central incisors. The sides of the tongue touch the inside of the upper teeth.

Description

The /z/ is produced when the voiced air stream from the larynx is modified by the a narrow, shallow orifice created by the slightly downward deflect of a grooved tongue. The air stream creates a frictionlike sound as it passes the edge of the teeth.

Spellings

z as in zinc, dozen, and breeze
zz as in puzzle
s as in eyes
x as in exit

Comments

1. The second acceptable acoustic variation of the alveolar /z/ is called the dental /z/. In the production of this phoneme, the tongue tip is raised toward the alveolar ridge, thus deflecting the air stream upward.
2. The /z/ was first pronounced in Middle English but spelled as s. The /z/ was used only in Biblical names and French loanwords.
3. The /z/ is used to denote regular plurals in words ending in voiced consonants.
4. Some words use the /s/ and /z/ interchangeably in pronunciation depending of the context. Two common examples are *use* [juz] or [jus] and *close* [kloz] or [klos].
5. The production of the /z/ frequently affected by dentition.

Monosyllabic Word Practice

1. Transcribe each of the following words into phonetics:

is	buzz	ties
toys	lays (laze)	zip
zone	jazz	tease
Zen	zoo	lose
dolls	saws	goods
cows		

2. Count and record the number of phonemes per word.
3. Label each phoneme using the terms CV, VC, CVC, and so on.
4. Which of the 11 vowels and 3 major diphthongs are not represented in the word practice?
5. Can you think of a monosyllabic word that has /z/ in the initial or final position and contains the vowels or diphthongs not represented?

Reading Practice

1. Read each of the words written in phonetics aloud.
2. Write each of the words in orthography noting various spellings:

/aɪz/	/zæp/	/kloz/
/æz/	/hoz/	/dez/

/ʃ/—ESH

Parameters

The /ʃ/ is a voiceless, postalveolar fricative.

Production

1. The vocal folds are open.
2. The velopharyngeal port is closed.
3. The mandible is slightly depressed.
4. The lips are spread.
5. The tongue is elevated, slightly retracted, and flattened. The tongue tip lies slightly below the hard palate behind the alveolar ridge. The sides of the tongue touch the inside of the upper teeth in the premolar and molar areas.

Description

The /ʃ/ is produced when the air stream from the lungs is modified by the a wide, shallow orifice created by a flattened tongue. The air stream creates a frictionlike sound as it passes between the teeth and lips.

Spellings

sh as in shoe, bushel, and wish
s as in sugar
c as in ocean
ss as in fissure
ch as in crochet
tion as in fiction
sch as in schwa

Comments

1. The /ʃ/ sound is frequently misarticulated. It is highly affected by dentition.
2. The /ʃ/ is one phoneme, although it is spelled frequently as the digraph sh.
3. The esh, called the long s, was used in Old English for the s. The use of the long s as a variation of s continued until the 1800s.

Monosyllabic Word Practice

1. Transcribe each of the following words into phonetics:

sheep	ship	shape
flesh	shop	shut
shy	shout	should
shoot	chic	shawl
show	shock	mash

2. Count and record the number of phonemes per word.
3. Label each phoneme using the terms CV, VC, CVC, and so on.
4. Which of the 11 vowels and 3 major diphthongs are not represented in the word practice?
5. Can you think of a monosyllabic word that has /ʃ/ in the initial or final position and contains the vowels or diphthongs not represented?

Reading Practice

1. Read each of the words written in phonetics aloud.
2. Write each of the words in orthography noting various spellings:

/ʃæg/	/ʃev/	/ʃɑt/
/ʃʌʃ/	/ʃon/	/ʃʊk/

/ʒ/—YOGH

Parameters

The /ʒ/ is a voiced, postalveolar fricative.

Production

1. The vocal folds are vibrating.
2. The velopharyngeal port is closed.
3. The mandible is slightly depressed.
4. The lips are spread.
5. The tongue is elevated, slightly retracted, and flattened. The tongue tip lies slightly below the hard palate behind the alveolar ridge. The sides of the tongue touch the inside of the upper teeth in the premolar and molar areas.

Description

The /ʒ/ is produced when the voiced air stream from the larynx is modified by the a wide, shallow orifice created by a flattened tongue. The air stream creates a frictionlike sound as it passes between the teeth and lips.

Spellings

z as in azure
s as in vision
g as in garage

Comments

1. The /ʒ/ sound is frequently misarticulated. It is highly affected by dentition.
2. The /ʒ/ is a French sound and does not appear initially in GAP.
3. The yogh was used as a plosive to represent the /g/ and the glide /g/ in Old English. During Middle English the /ʒ/ was used as a glide. In Modern English the use of the /ʒ/ as a fricative in French loanwords began.
4. This is one of the last sounds learned by children and is infrequently used in GAP.

Monosyllabic Word Practice

1. Transcribe the following words into phonetics:

rouge   beige   loge

luge

2. Count and record the number of phonemes per word.
3. Label each phoneme using the terms CV, VC, CVC, and so on.
4. Which of the 11 vowels and 3 major diphthongs are not represented in the word practice?
5. Can you think of a monosyllabic word that has /ʒ/ in the initial or final position and contains the vowels or diphthongs not represented?

Reading Practice

There are only a few common words with the /ʒ/ phoneme at the monosyllabic word level and they are included in the practice just given.

/h/—LOWER-CASE H

Parameters

The /h/ is voiceless glottal fricative.

Production

1. The vocal folds are open.
2. The velopharyngeal port is closed.
3. The /h/ will assume the mandible, lips, and tongue posture of the adjacent vowel.

Description

The /h/ is unique in that it assumes the posture of the adjacent vowel.

Spellings

h as in him or behind
wh as in who

Comments

1. In some situations, the /h/ many not be completely voiceless rather just weakened.
2. The /h/ does not appear in the final position of words in GAP.
3. The /h/ is silent in numerous spellings such as the words *oh, hour,* and *night.*

Monosyllabic Word Practice

1. Transcribe each of the following words into phonetics:

heat	whom	hit
hate	hen	hat
hook	hope	haunt
hut	hide	hot

2. Count and record the number of phonemes per word.
3. Label each phoneme using the terms CV, VC, CVC, and so on.
4. Which of the 11 vowels and 3 major diphthongs are not represented in the word practice?
5. Can you think of a monosyllabic word that has /h/ in the initial or final position and contains the vowels or diphthongs not represented?

Reading Practice

1. Read each of the words written in phonetics aloud.
2. Write each of the words in orthography noting various spellings:

/hæd/	/hɔlt/	/hil/
/hɑb/	/hut/	/haɪv/

Review Questions

1. What are the four pairs of fricative cognates?
2. What is the single fricative phoneme?
3. How are the high and low frequencies combined to form the /f/?
4. Historically, what phoneme was used instead of /v/?
5. What are the names of the /θ/ and the /ð/?
6. What is the weakest phoneme?
7. Why is the theta phoneme so difficult to produce for ESL speakers?
8. What is a common AAE substitution pattern?
9. Why is the eth one of the last phonemes mastered by children?
10. What is the second acceptable variation of the /s/ and /z/?
11. What is the most frequently used consonant in GAP?
12. Syntactically, what do the /s/ and /z/ phonemes produce?
13. Why is the /s/ so frequently misarticulated?
14. Historically, when was the /z/ used?
15. Historically, the esh was a variation of what?
16. What language does the yogh come from?
17. What is the least frequently used phoneme?
18. Does the /h/ appear in the final position in GAP?

Exercises

1. Transcribe the following cognates into phonetics and label the phonological pattern:

/f/ and /v/

fine	vine
fat	vat
fault	vault
few	view
file	vile
safe	save
fan	van
feign	vain
fest	vest
fin	vin

/θ/ and /ð/

cloth	clothe
breath	breathe
bath	bathe
sooth	soothe
booth	booths
thigh	thy
teeth	teethe
swath	swathe
lath	lathe
loath	loathe

/s/ and /z/

Sue (sue)	zoo
sip	zip
fleece	flees
bus	buzz
loose	lose
see	Z
sax	Zach's
sane	zane
sing	zing
sink	zinc

/ʃ/ and /ʒ/

There are not enough monosyllabic words /ʒ/ to include this drill.

2. Transcribe the following contrasts into phonetics and label the phonological pattern (note some contrasts are limited in number and others are not possible):

/f/ and /ʃ/

fin	shin
feet	sheet
puff	pus
phone	shone
half	hash
fed	shed
fell	shell
fun	shun
whiff	wish
foe	show

/f/ and /s/

fight	site (sight)
faint (feint)	saint
foot	soot
feet	seat
fought	sought
foil	soil
goof	goose
fee	see
fax	sax
fox	socks

/f/ and /θ/

(The /f/ for the /θ/ is a common substitution found in AAE.)

laugh	lath
fin	thin
fought	thought
oaf	oath
loaf	loath
feign	thane
deaf	death
thief	fief
myth	miff
with	whiff

/θ/ and /ʃ/

froth	frosh
thigh	shy
thaw	shaw
thank	shank
hath	hash
bath	bash
thin	shin
with	wish
lath	lash

/θ/ and /s/

(Many ESL speakers substitute the /s/ for the /θ/. The substitution of the /θ/ for the /s/ is called an interdental lisp.)

thin	sin
thumb	sum
thick	sick
thank	sank
thaw	saw
path	pass
theme	seam (seem)
faith	face
thigh	sigh
bath	bass

/s/ and /ʃ/

(The substitution of the /s/ for the /ʃ/ is a common error made by children.)

seep	sheep
seat	sheet
sip	ship
sigh	shy
sock	shock
mass	mash
sane	Shane
sin	shin
see	she
sue (Sue)	shoe

/h/ and /f/

heat	feet
hate	fate
hit	fit
hat	fat
hone	phone
hall	fall
hang	fang
hoax	folks
head	fed

/h/ and /s/

heat	seat
hit	sit
hat	sat
hope	soap
hide	side
high (hi)	sigh
hick	sick
Hank	sank
he	see
hex	sex

/h/ and /ʃ/

hook	shook
heat	sheet

hut	shut
hot	shot
Hank	shank
he	she
high	shy
hone	shone
heap	sheep
head	shed

/h/ and /θ/

had	Thad
hatch	thatch
high (hi)	thigh
hum	thumb
Hank	thank
hick	thick
hug	thug
haw	thaw
hump	thump

/v/ and /z/

| vets | zest |
| voom | zoom |

/v/ and /ð/

| van | than |
| vat | that |

vie	thy
vine	thine
vow	thou

/z/ and /ʒ/

bays	beige
rues	rogue
lows	loge

/ʒ/ and /ð/

beige	bathe
loge	loathe

/z/ and /ð/

(The use of the /ð/ for the /z/ is a form of an interdental lisp.)

Zen	then
bays	bathe
Zee	thee
seas	seethe
close	clothe
tease	teethe
breeze	breathe

APPROXIMANTS

The approximants include /ɹ/, /l/, and the /j/. An approximant sound is produced by the proximity of two articulators without turbulent air.

The lateral approximant /l/ possesses all the features of the other approximants with the addition of the lateral flow of the air stream from the oral cavity.

/ɹ/—TURNED R

Parameters

The /ɹ/ is a voiced, alveolar approximant.

Production

1. The vocal folds are vibrating.
2. The velopharyngeal port is closed.
3. The mandible is slightly depressed.
4. The lips are spread.
5. The tongue is elevated, slightly retracted, and pointing toward the roof of the mouth. The tongue tip lies slightly below the hard palate behind the alveolar ridge. The sides of the tongue touch the inside of the upper teeth in the premolar and molar areas.

Description

The /ɹ/ is produced when the voiced air stream from the larynx is modified by the close approximation of the tongue tip to the hard palate directly behind the alveolar ridge.

Spellings

r as in red
rh as in rhythmic
wr as in write
str as in stray
scr as in scrap
spr as in spring

Comments

1. The /ɹ/ phoneme is one part of a large group of sounds that form the r spelling in American-English. Chapter 7 provides more information on variations of the r orthographic symbol.
2. The voiced, alveolar approximant is found only in beginning positions of words and in the /wr/, and /str/, /skr/, and /spr/ clusters. In other initial position clusters the /ɹ/ often becomes voiceless.
3. Prior to 1989, the IPA used the lower case r /r/ as the symbol for the initial r.

Monosyllabic Word Practice

1. Transcribe each of the following words into phonetics:

rind   read (reed)   rid

raid   red   ran

roost	road (rode)	wrought
rock	rub	rhyme
wrist	script	rod
string	spry	rook
Roy	row	

2. Count and record the number of phonemes per word.
3. Label each phoneme using the terms CV, VC, CVC, and so on.
4. Which of the 11 vowels and 3 major diphthongs are not represented in the word practice?
5. Can you think of a monosyllabic word that has /ɹ/ in the initial or final position and contains the vowels or diphthongs not represented?

Reading Practice

1. Read each of the words written in phonetics aloud.
2. Write each of the words in orthography noting various spellings:

| /ɹev/ | /ɹaɪz/ | /ɹip/ |
| /ɹɪm/ | /ɹæt/ | /ɹol/ |

/j/—LOWER-CASE J

Parameters

The /j/ is a voiced, palatal approximant.

Production

1. The vocal folds are vibrating.
2. The velopharyngeal port is closed.
3. The mandible is depressed.
4. The lips are spread.
5. The tongue tip is pointing downward and initially resting behind the lower incisors. The tongue tip is raised toward the alveolar ridge as the following vowels is produced.

Description

The /j/ is produced when the voiced air stream from the larynx is modified by the movement of the tongue tip from behind the lower incisors to the alveolar ridge during coarticulation.

Spellings

y as in yard
i as in union
u as in use

Comments

1. The /j/ sound is never spelled as a j in GAP. The /j/ is a short sound and must be released by a vowel.
2. The /j/ is often intrusive in words having two adjacent vowels as in *union* [ˈjun jən].

Monosyllabic Word Practice

1. Transcribe each of the following words into phonetics:

ye	yip	yeah
use	yak	yolk
yet	yacht	yon
yawn	few	yowl

2. Count and record the number of phonemes per word.
3. Label each phoneme using the terms CV, VC, CVC, and so on.
4. Which of the 11 vowels and 3 major diphthongs are not represented in the word practice?
5. Can you think of a monosyllabic word that has /j/ in the initial or final position and contains the vowels or diphthongs not represented?

Reading Practice

1. Read each of the words written in phonetics aloud.
2. Write each of the words in orthography noting various spellings:

/jɛlp/	/jæŋk/	/jɛs/
/jʌm/	/jɪld/	/jæm/

/l/—LOWER-CASE L

Parameters

The /l/ is a voiced, alveolar, lateral approximant.

Production

1. The vocal folds are vibrating.
2. The velopharyngeal port is closed.

3. The mandible is slightly depressed.
4. The lips are spread.
5. The tongue is elevated, slightly retracted, and pointing toward the roof of the mouth. The tongue tip lightly touches lightly the alveolar ridge. The sides of the tongue are dropped and the air stream is emitted laterally.

Description

The /l/ is produced when the voiced air stream from the larynx is modified by the tongue tip being place on the alveolar ridge. The sides of the tongue blade dropped to allow lateral emission of the voiced air stream.

Spellings

l as in lie, dollar, and bell
ll as in fall
le as in apple
el as in kennel
sl as in isle
ln as in kiln
lm as in film
lt as in guilt
ld as in build
bl as in blithe
gl as in glee

Comments

1. The /l/ appears as a partially voiceless sound in /pl/, /kl/, /sl/, and /fl/ clusters in narrow transcription. The under-ring /l̥/ is placed under the symbol to indicated this.
2. The /l/ appears in numerous final position clusters.
3. The /l/ is silent in a series of common words such as *walk* [wɔk].
4. The /l/ influences the vowels preceding it.
5. The /l/ is the only phoneme that is produced by a lateral emission of the air stream from the oral cavity.

Monosyllabic Word Practice

1. Transcribe each of the following words into phonetics:

lee	limp	lay
left	lake	law
low	loose	look
luck	lats	like
aisle	lock	slide

field	bly	glide
owl	Lloyd	

2. Count and record the number of phonemes per word.
3. Label each phoneme using the terms CV, VC, CVC, and so on.
4. Which of the 11 vowels and 3 major diphthongs are not represented in the word practice?
5. Can you think of a monosyllabic word that has /l/ in the initial or final position and contains the vowels or diphthongs not represented?

Reading Practice

1. Read each of the words written in phonetics aloud.
2. Write each of the words in orthography noting various spellings:

/lʌmp/	/lænd/	/lɛnz/
/lɪt/	/lut/	/lis/

Review Questions

1. What is the symbol for the initial position r in GAP?
2. In what blends is the initial position r not voiceless?
3. What are some /ɹ/ clusters in which the r becomes voiceless?
4. What are some of the spellings for the /j/?
5. Think of two other words in which the /j/ is found.
6. Think of five final position /l/ blends.
7. In what /l/ blends is the /l/ partially voiced?
8. Think of two words in which the /l/ is silent.

Exercises

1. Transcribe the following contrasts into phonetics and label the phonological pattern (the /l/ for the /ɹ/ is a common substitution pattern in ESL speakers):

/ɹ/ and /l/

red	led
rock	lock
wrist	list
road	load

rook	look
rid	lid
row	low
rim	limb
rake	lake
ray	lay

/j/ and /ɹ/

yip	rip
yak	ack
yam	ram
yacht	rot
yen	wren
yap	rap
yet	Rhett
yank	rank
yon	Ron
young	rung

/l/ and /j/

(The /j/ for the /j/ and the reverse are common developmental errors.)

lee	ye
let	yet
lamb	yam
loose	use
lawn	yawn

lap	yap
lip	yip
lack	yak
lot	yacht
Lou	you

OTHER PHONEMES

This section is devoted to the five remaining phonemes commonly used in GAP. The combination phonemes /ʍ/ and /w/ are listed in the other symbols section of the IPA. The two affricate phonemes /t ʃ/ and /dʒ/ are also considered combination phonemes by the IPA. The remaining phoneme is the glottal. The glottal is a voiceless, glottal plosive. The glottal is unique in that it is nonphonemic in GAP. For this reason, it is included in this section rather than with the plosives.

Combination Phonemes /ʍ/ and /w/

/ʍ/—INVERTED W

Parameters

The /ʍ/ is a voiceless, labial-velar fricative.

Production

1. The vocal folds are open.
2. The velopharyngeal port is closed.
3. The mandible is slightly depressed.
4. The lips are rounded.
5. The tongue is neutral.

Description

The /ʍ/ is produced when the air stream from the lungs passes through the rounded lips creating a frictionlike quality.

Spellings

wh as in when and nowhere
wh as in why
w as in swim and twin

Comments

1. The /ʍ/ is a short duration phoneme but it is not an approximant.
2. The /w/ and /ʍ/ are not cognates.
3. There is no friction in the production of the /w/ but friction is present in the production of /ʍ/.
4. The /ʍ/ is used after the /s/, /t/, and /θ/ in consonant clusters.
5. The /ʍ/ has historically been transcribed as /hw/ and both phonemes were pronounced. During Middle English the hw spelling disappeared and was replaced by wh, w, or h. The use of the /ʍ/ is appropriately used in the broad transcription of most words beginning with the wh spelling. The /ʍ/ phoneme, however, is disappearing from common usage in GAP and is replaced by most speakers at the conversational level with the /w/. (Note that some words beginning with the wh spelling have a silent w such as in the word *who* /huː/.)

Monosyllabic Word Practice

1. Transcribe each of the following words into phonetics:

sweet   sweat   twine

whet   whip   when

why   what   whale

whey   while   which

thwack

2. Count and record the number of phonemes per word.
3. Label each phoneme using the terms CV, VC, CVC, and so on.
4. Which of the 11 vowels and 3 major diphthongs are not represented in the word practice?
5. Can you think of a monosyllabic word that has /ʍ/ in the initial or final position and contains the vowels or diphthongs not represented?

Reading Practice

1. Read each of the words written in phonetics aloud.
2. Write each of the words in orthography noting various spellings:

/ʍel/   /ʍaɪt/   /ʍɪsk/
/ʍaɪn/   /ʍiz/   /ʍit/

/w/—LOWER-CASE W

Parameters

The /w/ is a voiced, labial-velar approximant.

Production

1. The vocal folds are vibrating.
2. The velopharyngeal port is closed.
3. The mandible is slightly depressed.
4. The lips are rounded.
5. The tongue is neutral.

Description

The /w/ is produced when the voiced air stream from the larynx passes through the rounded lips and then coarticulates with the following vowel.

Spellings

w as in way and away
o as in once
dw as in dwell
gw as in Gwen

Comments

1. The /w/ is a short duration phoneme and must be released by a vowel.
2. The /w/ is often intrusive in the pronunciation of words having two adjacent vowels such as *chewing* [ˈtʃu wɪŋ].
3. The w is historically silent in wr clusters.
4. /w/ and /ʍ/ are not cognates. The /w/ has no friction.
5. The /w/ is not found in the final position of words in GAP.

Monosyllabic Word Practice

1. Transcribe each of the following words into phonetics:

we	win	way
wet	wow	wool
woke	walk	won(one)
was	wise	watt
once	woo	

2. Count and record the number of phonemes per word.
3. Label each phoneme using the terms CV, VC, CVC, and so on.
4. Which of the 11 vowels and 3 major diphthongs are not represented in the word practice?
5. Can you think of a monosyllabic word that has /w/ in the initial or final position and contains the vowels or diphthongs not represented?

6. What is the beginning phoneme you use when pronouncing the following words?

whack	whale	wheeze
wham	wharf	what
wheat	wheel	wheeze
when	where	while
white		

Reading Practice

1. Read each of the words written in phonetics aloud.
2. Write each of the words in orthography noting various spellings:

/wɑʃ/	/wed/	/wɛl/
/wɪt/	/wo/	/wʊlf/

Affricates

An affricate is a term applied to a sound sequence found in GAP consisting of a plosive followed by a homorganic fricative phoneme. The IPA recognizes combinations of phonemes such as /tʃ/, /dʒ/, /tθ/, /dð/, /ts/, and /dz/ by using a tie bar. The phonemes comprising the affricates /tʃ/ and /dʒ/ are considered by many phoneticians to have a special relationship that is not common to other consonant clusters. In GAP, the other affricates including /tθ/ (*eighth*) and /dð/ (*width*) and /ts/ (*pats*), /dz/ (*pads*) are considered by most authorities to be consonant clusters appearing only in the final position and generally related to syntactical aspects of the word such as forming the plural.

In the production of an affricate sound, the articulatory posture is that of the second sound with the influence of the stopping action of the plosive. The second sound is usually stronger acoustically. Only the /tʃ/ and /dʒ/ are covered in this section.

/tʃ/—T-ESH LIGATURE

Parameters

The /tʃ/ is a voiceless, alveolar-postalveolar fricative

Production

1. The vocal folds are open.
2. The velopharyngeal port is closed.
3. The mandible is slightly depressed.

4. The lips are spread.
5. The tongue is elevated, slightly retracted, and flattened. The tongue tip lies slightly below the hard palate behind the alveolar ridge. The sides of the tongue touch the inside of the upper teeth in the premolar and molar areas.

Description

The /t ʃ/ is produced when the air stream from the lungs is modified by a wide, shallow orifice created by a flattened tongue place behind the alveolar ridge. The breath stream is released slowly and with a pressure build up.

Spellings

ch as in chop, teacher, and march
tch as in kitchen
t(ure) as in fracture
t(u) as in natural
c as in cello

Comments

1. In very early Old English the /k/ was used for velar sound and c for palatal sounds. This original /k/ was used for what is now the /t ʃ/ sound. As time progressed the /k/ symbol was dropped and c had two positions. One position was used to represent the /k/ sound and one represented the back or guttural sound. This back guttural sound became the /t ʃ/ sound in Middle English but was often represented by the /h/ symbol.
2. The /t ʃ/ is an intrusive sound in words like *tension* [ˈtɛn tʃən].
3. The C wedge /č/ is an alternate symbol for the /t ʃ/ but it is not recognized by the IPA.

Monosyllabic Word Practice

1. Transcribe each of the following words into phonetics:

cheese	chin	chain
chop	match	chew
chunk	choke	chug
chalk	choose	chow
choice	check	child
change	latch	rich

2. Count and record the number of phonemes per word.
3. Label each phoneme using the terms CV, VC, CVC, and so on.

4. Which of the 11 vowels and 3 major diphthongs are not represented in the word practice?

5. Can you think of a monosyllabic word that has /t ʃ/ in the initial or final position and contains the vowels or diphthongs not represented?

Reading Practice

1. Read each of the words written in phonetics aloud.
2. Write each of the words in orthography noting various spellings:

/t ʃæmp/   /t ʃik/   /t ʃɪps/
/t ʃaɪv/   /t ʃæps/   /t ʃok/

/dʒ/—D-YOGH LIGATURE

Parameters

The /dʒ/ is a voiced, alveolar–postalveolar fricative

Production

1. The vocal folds are vibrating.
2. The velopharyngeal port is closed.
3. The mandible is slightly depressed.
4. The lips are spread.
5. The tongue is elevated, slightly retracted, and flattened. The tongue tip lies slightly below the hard palate behind the alveolar ridge. The sides of the tongue touch the inside of the upper teeth in the premolar and molar areas.

Description

The /dʒ/ is produced when the voiced air stream from the larynx is modified by a wide, shallow orifice created by a flattened tongue placed behind the alveolar ridge. The breath stream is released slowly and with a pressure build up.

Spellings

j as in jump and enjoy
dg as in edge
g as in age
dj as in adjourn
d as in gradual
gg as in exaggerate

Comments

1. The j wedge /ǰ/ is an alternate symbol of the /dʒ/, but it is not recognized by the IPA.

Monosyllabic Word Practice

1. Transcribe each of the following words into phonetics:

jeep	job	Jake
jell	jam	jump
joy	ledge	rage
jaw	huge	gin
jug	joke	

2. Count and record the number of phonemes per word.
3. Label each phoneme using the terms CV, VC, CVC, and so on.
4. Which of the 11 vowels and 3 major diphthongs are not represented in the word practice?
5. Can you think of a monosyllabic word that has /dʒ/ in the initial or final position and contains the vowels or diphthongs not represented?

Reading Practice

1. Read each of the words written in phonetics aloud.
2. Write each of the words in orthography noting various spellings:

/dʒus/	/dʒɑg/	/dʒɪlt/
/dʒɛm/	/dʒɪm/	/dʒed/

/ʔ/—GLOTTAL

Parameters

The /ʔ/ is a voiceless, glottal plosive.

Production

1. The vocal folds are open.
2. The velopharyngeal port is closed.

Description

The air stream from the lungs is stopped at the glottis.

Comments

1. The /ʔ/ is nonphonemic in GAP. More information on the glottal is available in chapter 6.
2. The glottal is also used by children learning the language.

Review Questions

1. Are the /w/ and the /ʍ/ cognates? Which of the two are produced with friction?
2. Is /w/ or /ʍ/ disappearing from use? Why?
3. Define affricate.
4. What are the two most common affricates? What are the four least common?
5. Historically, what sound is used for the /t ʃ/?
6. What is significant about the glottal phoneme?

Exercises

1. Transcribe the following cognates into phonetics and label the phonological pattern:

/t ʃ/ and /dʒ/

cheap	jeep
chain	Jane (Jayne)
chug	jug
choke	joke
chin	gin
chunk	junk
chip	gyp
chest	jest
chess	Jess
chill	Jill

2. Transcribe the following contrasts into phonetics and label the phonological patterns:

/w/ and /ʍ/

whet	wet
whey	way
which	witch
whine	wine

whit	wit
whack	Wac
white	Wight
Whig	wig
whiz	wiz

EXERCISES

1. Transcribe the following words into phonetics and label the phonological pattern. (These words often sound similar in an individual with a denasal voice quality. Note how voice quality can interfere with intelligibility.):

/b/ and /m/

bake	make
bee	me
bay	may (May)
boat	moat
boot	moot
beet (beat)	meat
bat	mat
rub	rum
lab	lamb
bean	mean

/d/ and /n/

dine	sign
deed	need
deck	neck
dough (doe)	no (know)

done	none
dot	not
bid	bin
mad	man
down	noun
odd	on

/g/ and /ŋ/

wig	wing
rig	ring
tug	tongue
lug	lung
big	bing
bog	bong
kin	king
sprig	spring
sin	sing
swig	swing

2. Transcribe the following words into phonetics and label the phonological pattern (the /b/ for the /v/, /p/ for the /f/, /w/ for the /l/, and /w/ for the /ɹ/ are common developmental errors):

/b/ and /v/

ban	van
bat	vat
base	vase
bend	vend

boat	vote
best	vest
bet	vet
bile	vial (vile)
Gabe	gave
boil	voile

/p/ and /f/

pad	fad
pace	face
pan	fan
pin	fin
pit	fit
pine	fine
pond	fond
pull	full
pun	fun
pool	fool

/w/ and /l/

woo	Lou
wet	let
wed	led (lead)
wake	lake
way	lay
win	Lynn

wean	lean
wax	lacks
we (wee)	lee (Lee)
wag	lag

/w/ and /ɹ/

won	run
wed	red
wok	rock
way	ray
wet	Rhett
wad	rod
wade	raid
wake	rake
wing	ring
wig	rig

3. Transcribe the following words and label the phonological pattern (in addition to the /s/ for the /θ/ substitution mentioned in the section on fricatives, other common ESL errors patterns are /t/ for /θ/, /d/ for /ð/, /v/ for /w/, and /v/ for /ʍ/.

/t/ and /θ/

theme	team (teem)
thank	tank
thick	tick (tic)
thin	tin
thigh	tie
thug	tug

both	boat
tooth	toot
oath	oat
myth	mitt

/ð/ and /d/

seethe	seed
than	Dan
thee	Dee
then	den
they	day
scythe	side
thine	dine
thy	die (dye)
tithe	tide
writhe	ride

/v/ and /w/

veal	we'll
vent	went
vest	west
vet	wet
vise	wise
vow	wow
veil	wail
Vince	wince

/v/ and /ʍ/

vile	while
veal	wheel
vim	whim
veil	whale
view	whew
vie	why

4. Transcribe the following contrasts into phonetics and label the phonological pattern (these are uncommon substitution patterns):

/l/ and /n/

lack	knack
lame	name
lap	nap
look	nook
licks	mix
lip	nip
loose	news
low	no
lock	knock
life	knife

/j/ and /w/

yet	wet
yell	well
yak	Wac
yes	Wes

yoke	woke
yeah	way (weigh)

/j/ and /ʍ/

you	whew
yelp	whelp
yip	whip
yet	whet
Yac	whack
yeah	whey

/dʒ/ and /j/

gip	yip
gel	yell
jam	yam
Jack	yak
jay	yeah
jaw	yaw
Jen	yen
joke	yoke
John (john)	yon
jot	yacht

5. Transcribe the following contrasts into phonetics and label the phonological pattern (consider the history of the sounds as you transcribe them):

/h/ and /w/

heap	weap
hall	wall

hay	way
hit	wit
hock	wok
how	wow
who	woo
hack	wack
hag	wag
haste	waist

/h/ and /ʍ/

heat	wheat
help	whelp
hi (high)	why
heap	weep
hen	when
heel	wheel
hut	what
hit	whit
height	white
him	whim

6. Transcribe the following contrasts into phonetics and label the phonological pattern:

/ʃ/ and /tʃ/

leash	leech
shaw	chaw
sheet	cheat

sheep	cheap (cheep)
she's	cheese
shoe	chew
shin	chin
ship	chip
shop	chop
shucks	Chuck's

/t/ and /t ʃ/

time	chime
tap	chap
taste	chaste
tease	cheese
test	chest
two (to or too)	chew
tide	chide
tin	chin
tip	chip
bat	batch

7. Transcribe the following affricate contrasts into phonetics and label the phonological pattern:

/dʒ/ and /dz/

rage	raids
age	aids
budge	buds
edge	Ed's

ridge	rids
wage	wades
wedge	weds
hedge	heads
siege	seeds
Midge	mids

/t ʃ/ and /ts/

beach	beats
blotch	blots
coach	coats
each	eats
hatch	hats
it	chits
much	mutts
niche	knits
patch	pats
witch	wits

NOTES

Chapter 6

Single Phoneme and Phonological Development

PHONEME DEVELOPMENT

Infants begin making sounds at birth. These early sounds are cries that can be differentiated by a familiar ear. As the infant continues to mature, cooing and babbling noises develop into consonant and vowel sounds. These early preconsonant and prevowel sounds gradually become shaped into words. Although research indicates that some phonemes are present in neonates, phoneme development for purposes of speech generally begins between the first and second birthdays. Phoneme development is influenced by the child's environment; his or her physical, motor, and intellectual capabilities; and the child's need for communication.

THE DEVELOPMENT OF VOWELS

Vowels begin to develop from random sounds produced by infants as young as 2 months. At 2 months, the /ɛ/, /ɪ/, and /ʌ/ vowels are frequently identified in cooing patterns. These vowels fade after several months and are not consistently used again until after 30 months of age. At the same time that the /ɛ/, /ɪ/, and /ʌ/ are fading, the front vowels /i/, /e/, and /æ/ are appearing. These three front vowels, along with the back vowels /ɑ/, /ɔ/, /o/, /ʊ/, and /u/, are consistently used and mastered over the next 2 years (Irwin & Chen, 1946). As the first words appear between the first and second birthdays, CV patterns consisting of /ɑ/, /æ/, and /o/ dominate speech patterns.

THE DEVELOPMENT OF CONSONANTS

Although numerous researchers have studied the concept of phoneme acquisition, the two most significant recent studies have been completed by Smit, Hand, Frelinger, Bernthal, and Bird (1990) and Sander (1972). Although completed more than 20 years ago, Sander's information provides the most clinically applicable

130

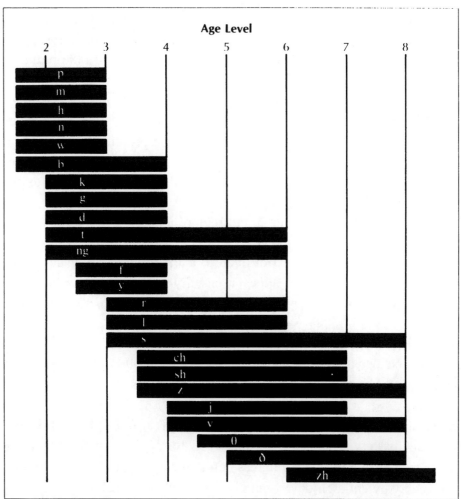

FIG. 6.1. Sander's norms (reprinted by permission of the American Speech-Language-Hearing Association).

data. Sander included in his information a range of ages associated with the development of various consonant phonemes (see Fig. 6.1).

According to Sander, the first consonant phonemes to develop are the /p/, /m/, /h/, /n/, /w/, and /b/. These phonemes begin to develop before the age of 2, and all but the /b/ are mastered by age 3. The /b/ is not mastered until age 4. These phonemes consist of two highly visible plosives—the /p/ and the /b/—two nasal sounds—the /n/ and the /m/—and the fricative /h/. These phonemes require little adjustment of the vocal tract, and the approximant /w/ is highly visible and similar to the bilabial plosives.

The next group of consonant phonemes to develop includes the /k/, /g/, /d/, /t/, and /ŋ/. Each of these phonemes begins to develop at age 2. The plosives /k/, /g/, and /d/ are mastered at age 4, whereas the plosive /t/ and the nasal /ŋ/ are not mastered until age 6. Considering the first two groups of phonemes, it is obvious that plosives and nasals are common in a child's early vocabulary. Although it is possible for a child to have difficulty with the pronunciation of any phoneme, most of these early phonemes, except perhaps /k/, are not problematic. Young children's frequent substitution of the /t/ for the /k/ is called **velar fronting.** This substitution is possibly due to either the lack of visibility of the /k/ or poor musculature control of the velum. The delayed mastery of the /t/ is also associated with the syntactic use of the /t/ as a past tense marker.

The later mastery of the /ŋ/ is associated with its syntactic role forming the present progressive and the fact that the phonological rules of American-English do not allow for the production of the /ŋ/ in the initial position of words. Because children generally master the target phoneme in the initial position of words first, the /ŋ/ would necessarily be mastered later in the developmental sequence.

The /f/ and /j/ phonemes begin to develop before the age of 3 and are mastered by the age of 4. The /f/ is the first fricative phoneme to be mastered, probably because of its visible place of articulation. Some children substitute the /p/ for the /f/ at an early age. This error represents a manner of articulation error that is common only in children less than age 4. The /j/ is the first approximant phoneme to be mastered and it requires a neutral position of the articulators. Because this phoneme is easy to produce, it is often used as a substitute for more difficult phonemes.

The /ɹ/, /l/ and /s/ begin to develop at age 3, but require a lengthy period of time before mastery is accomplished. The /ɹ/ and the /l/ are mastered at age 6, whereas the /s/ is not fully mastered age 8. These three phonemes are often considered the most difficult to learn and thus are usually the most frequently mispronounced. The consonantal /ɹ/, which appears only in the initial position of words or syllables in GAP, is often replaced by the /w/ or the /j/. Both of these phonemes are easier to produce. In addition, the /ɹ/ and the /l/ are very complex phonemes and the various allophonic variations make their mastery difficult. The /s/ phoneme requires well-coordinated use of the intrinsic and extrinsic muscles of the tongue. This sophisticated phoneme also uses a higher frequency (about 4000 Hz.) than any other phoneme. The phonemes /ɹ/, /l/, and /s/ are also found in initial position CC contexts more often than any other consonant phoneme.

The /tʃ/, /ʃ/, and /z/ are the next phonemes to develop. A 3 ½-year-old child can produce these phonemes in selected situations, but mastery is not achieved until age 7 for the /tʃ/ and /ʃ/ and age 8 for the /z/. The affricate /tʃ/ requires the mastery of two phonemes before it can be produced. Thus, the /ʃ/ and /tʃ/ are often used interchangeably by children developing speech. Although the /z/ is used in some vocabulary words, its primary role in the English language is as a plural marker. This syntactic mastery is not achieved until a later age.

The /dʒ/ and the /v/ are the next group of phonemes to develop. These phonemes begin to develop at age 4 and are mastered by ages 6 and 7, respectively. The /dʒ/ is an affricate that requires mastery of two phonemes. Because the /ʒ/ is not yet mastered by many children, the production of /dʒ/ is often difficult. Substitution of /b/ for /v/ is common in children up to the age of 5 or 6 because the /v/ is not commonly used.

The /θ/ begins to develop before age 4 and is mastered by age 7, whereas the /ð/ begins to develop at age 5 and is mastered by age 8. The /θ/ is a weak phoneme, but its visibility and interdental tongue positions make it a common substitution for the more difficult but frequently appearing /s/ phoneme. The substitution of the /θ/ for the /s/ is often called an interdental lisp. The /ð/ is used primarily in function words such as *the, them,* and *these.* Because the use of function words is directly related to the development of the noun and verb phrases, the use of /ð/ increases as the complexity of the phrase increases.

The last two phonemes to develop are the /ʒ/ and the /ʍ/. The /ʒ/ begins to develop at age 6 and is mastered after age 8. The /ʍ/ begins to develop at age 6 and is not mastered until after age 9. The /ʒ/ is one of the last phonemes to be mastered because of its lack of frequency in early vocabulary words and its presence in only the medial and final position of words. The /ʍ/ is often replaced by the /w/ in conversational speech.

VARIATIONS IN THE DEVELOPMENT OF SINGLE PHONEMES

Not all children develop the consonants with ease at the target age. Some children experience a slower than normal development of the phonemes, whereas others exhibit common developmental patterns of substitution, omission, and distortion. **Substitution** is the replacing of one phomene for another, such as /b/ for the /v/ resulting in *ban* [bæn] for *van* [væn]. **Omission** is when a sound is omitted from the word. The endings are omitted from the word, such as *lef* [lɛf] for *left* [lɛft]. **Distortion** occurs when the phoneme is produced using an incorrect allophonic variation such as [s̃un] for [sun].

Children substitute, omit, or distort phonemes for a variety of reasons including developmental, hearing, physical, or dental limitations; imitation; or problems learning the language's rule system.

Developmental limitation is one of the most common causes of phoneme errors. The following are common developmental substitutions: /p/f/, /t/k/, /b/v/, /f/v/, /f/θ/, /w/ɹ/, /w/l/, /j/l/, /l/j/, /θ /s/, /n/ŋ/, and /w/ʍ/. These are probably used by children because one phoneme is easier to produce than another.

PHONOLOGICAL DEVELOPMENT

In addition to learning the phonemes of the language, distinct syllable patterns begin to develop shortly before the end of a child's first year or as soon as two phonemes are produced consecutively. The earliest patterns consist of CV *hi* [haɪ] or VC *up* [ʌp] patterns. These early patterns develop into CVCV *mama* [ˈmʌ mə] reduplication patterns or CVCV *cookie* [ˈkuki]. During this developmental time frame, a few CVC cat [kæt] patterns also develop, but in most cases the final consonant is omitted during the production (Owens, 1996).

Phonological processes are a series of patterns used by children to simplify adult speech. These patterns are used because the child does not yet have the capacity to produce adult speech. These patterns seem to be innate in all children but do not always develop at the same rate. Phonological patterns consist of syllable combinations, cluster combinations, and CV combinations. These processes account for patterns of substitutions, omissions, and additions present in developing speech between the ages of 2 and 5 (Creaghead, Newman, & Secord, 1989).

BASIC TERMINOLOGY

Some of the terms used in phonology differ from terms used by the IPA. To avoid confusion, the following definitions are provided.

Assimilation: The effect of one phoneme on another in a sequence of phonemes.
Backing: The production of consonants near the velar or glottal area.
Cluster: Two or more consonant phonemes in a sequence without being separated by a vowel.
Final consonants: The last consonant in the word or syllable.
Fronting: The production of consonants near the lips or the central and lateral incisors.
Initial consonant: The first consonant in the syllable or word.
Liquid: Term referring to the /l/ or /ɹ/ phonemes or allophones.
Medial consonant: The consonant in the medial position of the word.
Palatal: The area on the roof of the mouth that covers the maxillary bone.

Reduplication: The repetition of a CV syllable.
Stop: Another term for a plosive.
Stridency: A term used to apply to the consonants /s, z, f, v, ʒ, tʃ, dʒ/.

PHONOLOGICAL PROCESSES

There are numerous systems of phonological processes available for consideration. (It is not within the scope of this volume to examine numerous phonological processing systems in detail, but a brief overview is included.) According to Khan and Lewis (1986), there are 15 key phonological processes (12 occur as a part of normal development and 3 are not developmental in nature) and 15 less common phonological processes. (It is important to note that considerable interaction occurs among the processes. Those listed here are the pure forms.) The processes according to Khan and Lewis are as follow here.

Processes Associated With Normal Phonological Development

Deletion of final consonants: The final consonant in a word or syllable is deleted changing the syllable shape from CVC *bag* [bæg] to CV ([bæ]), CCVC *stop* [stɑp] to CCV [stɑ], or CVCC *box* [bɑks] to CV [bɑ]. The syllable changes from a closed to an open syllable.

Initial voicing: The use of the voiced consonant in place of a voiceless consonant in the initial position of the word or syllable. In the purest form, the child substitutes the cognate, for example, *dog* [dɔg] becomes [tɔg]. It is also considered initial consonant voicing when other processes are added and the child substitutes a voice consonant with a different place or manner of articulation, such as when *dog* [dɔg] becomes [gɔg].

Syllable reduction: One or more syllables in the word are deleted, such as when *library* ['laɪ ˌbɹɛɹi] becomes ['laɪ ˌbɛɹɨ].

Palatal fronting: The place of articulation is changed from the postalveolar area to the alveolar area, such as when *ship* [ʃɪp] becomes [sɪp].

Deaffrication: The stop part of the affricate is deleted. The word *cheek* [tʃik] becomes [ʃik].

Velar fronting: The place of articulation of the velar phonemes is shifted to the alveolar area. The word *cap* [kæp] becomes [tæp].

Consonant harmony: If the word has two or more consonants, the consonants are produced with the same place of articulation, such as when *cup* [kʌp] becomes [pʌp].

Stridency deletion: The stridency consonant is either deleted, as when *sun* [sʌn] becomes [ʌn], or is replaced with a glottal, as when *chip* [tʃɪp] becomes [ʔɪp].

Stopping of fricatives and affricates: This is when a stop consonant is substituted for a fricative. For example, the word *thank* [θæŋk] becomes [pæŋk]. When an affricate is stopped, only the plosive component of the affricate is produced, such as when [tʃɪn] becomes [tɪn].

Cluster simplification: One or more of the consonants in a CC or CCC context in any position of the word is deleted or a schwa is inserted, for example, *lamp* [læmp] becomes [læm].

Final devoicing: The voicing is deleted on the final consonant in the word or syllable. The result is usually the production of the voiceless cognate, such as when *bud* [bʌd] becomes [bʌt].

Liquid simplification—gliding of liquids: The liquid phonemes /l/ and /ɹ/ are produced as /w/ and /j/, for example, *light* [laɪt] becomes [waɪt].

Gliding of fricatives: Any fricative phoneme is produced as a /j/ or /w/, for example *five* [faɪv] becomes [jaɪv]. (This process is not very common.)

Vocalization of liquids: A vowel is produced instead of the final /l/ in an unstressed syllable or the /ɚ/, which is found only in unstressed syllables, for example, *flower* ['flaʊ wɚ] becomes ['flaʊ wə].

Processes That Are Nondevelopmental

These processes are not developmental and represent a phonological error at all ages.

Deletion of initial consonants: The first consonant in the word or syllable is deleted, such as when *top* [tɑp] becomes [ɑp].

Glottal replacement: A glottal is used to replace a consonant or a consonant cluster usually in the medial position of the word, for example, *sleeping* ['slip ɪŋ] becomes ['sliʔ ɪŋ].

Backing to velars: This is when any consonant is produced as a velar phoneme or an /h/, such as when *up* [ʌp] becomes [ʌk].

Ingram (1976) divided the phonological processes into three general categories: **syllable structure processes** such as final consonant deletion, **assimilatory processes** such as final consonant devoicing, and **substitution processes** such as stopping of fricatives and affricates. Grunwell (1982) listed nine processes that are common in the speech of children between ages 2 and 5. These processes are **weak syllable deletion, final consonant deletion, reduplication, consonant harmony, cluster reduction, stopping, fronting, gliding,** and **context sensitive voicing**.

Although phonological processes are used primarily by children learning the language and diminish over the first 5 years, they can also be identified in the speech patterns of adults. In using these various processes individual variations become part of a speech pattern. These processes are not rules but are often used consistently in conversational speech.

Phonological Rules/Phonotactics

Phonotactics are the rules that govern the combinations and ordering of phonemes in a syllable or a word. There are 16 phonological syllable patterns used in GAP (Creaghead, Newman, & Secord, 1989). Note the V can also appear as a word in GAP making the number of patterns 17. Following is a list of the syllables and an example for each.

One phoneme pattern	V	I [aɪ], oh [o]
Two phoneme patterns	VC	on [ɑn], it [ɪt]
	CV	be [bi], see [si]
Three phoneme patterns	CVC	dog [dθg], cat [kæt]
	CCV	tree [tɹi], ski [ski]
	VCC	its [ɪts], eats [its]
Four phoneme patterns	CCVC	slab [slæb]
		bread [bɹɛd]
	CCCV	stray [stɹe]
		spree [spɹi]

	VCCC	asked [æskt]
	CVCC	desk [dɛsk]
		fist [fɪst]
Five phoneme patterns	CCVCC	brown [bɹaʊn]
		spunk [spʌŋk]
	CCCVC	street [stɹit]
		strap [stɹæp]
	CVCCC	selves [sɛlvz]
		folds [foldz]
Six phoneme patterns	CCCVCC	strand [stɹænd]
		sprint [spɹɪnt]
	CCVCCC	stamps [stæmps]
		trenched [tɹɛntʃd]
	CVCCCC	sixths [sɪksθs]
Seven phoneme pattern	CCCVCCC	scrimped [skɹɪmpt]

Table 6.1 indicates order and frequency of occurrence of 14 of the 17 patterns in American-English (Faircloth, 1973).

Specific phoneme combinations are also governed by phonological rules. For example, the /ɹ/ is combined with the /b, f, g, k, p/ in the initial position but not with the /h, l, m, n, s, v, z/. Rules applying to /ɹ/, /l/, /ŋ/, and other factors that will influence articulation are discussed in chapters 7 and 9. For a complete list of the rules of the language see Ladefoged (1993).

TABLE 6.1
Order and Frequency of Occurrence of Phonologic Syllables in American English

Syllable	Percent (%)	Total
CV	32.40	
CVC	30.22	
VC	16.34	
V	8.11	
		87.07
CVCC	5.55	
CCVC	2.84	
CCV	2.64	
VCC	.72	
CCVCC	.60	
CCCVC	.24	
CCCVCC	.19	
CVCCC	.12	
CCVCCC	.02	
CCCV	.01	
		12.93
All syllables		100

Review Questions

1. When do infants begin to make sounds?
2. What types of sounds do infants produce?
3. At what age do vowels begin to appear?
4. What are the earliest vowels? Do these vowels continue to be used?
5. What are the front and back vowels that develop between 5 and 30 months?
6. What are the earliest CVs used by children?
7. Why do the /p/ and /b/ develop early? Why do the /n/ and /m/ develop early?
8. What plosive is often problematic? Why?
9. Why are the /t/ and the /ŋ/ mastered later?
10. What three consonants are most difficult to produce?
11. Why are the /t ʃ/ and /dʒ/ harder to produce?
12. Why do the /ʒ/ and /ʍ/ develop last?
13. What are the three common single phoneme developmental patterns used by children who are having trouble learning phonemes? Outline each briefly and give an example.
14. What are several common single phoneme developmental errors?
15. What are phonological processes?
16. Briefly define the following terms: initial consonant, medial consonant, final consonant, stridency, palatal, fronting, backing, cluster, stop, assimilation, reduplication, and liquid.
17. List and briefly explain the phonological processes according to Khan and Lewis.
18. What are phonotactics?
19. List the 17 syllable patterns that appear in GAP.
20. Which three syllable patterns occur most frequently?
21. Can all consonants be placed in clusters?

Exercises

1. Think of 10 early vocabulary words a young child might use. Using the chart in Fig. 1.1, identify the consonants and vowels used.
2. Using the same 10 vocabulary words, identify the phonological pattern of each.
3. Consulting Fig. 6.1, write the beginning and final age of acquisition for each consonant phoneme.
4. List and transcribe into phonetics three words for each of the 17 syllable patterns.
5. List 20 possible CC combinations

NOTES

PART II
STRESS AND THEORY

Chapter 7

Coarticulation

The influence of context on a particular phoneme is well documented. It is important to remember this interaction effect when transcribing phonemes in conversational speech. **Coarticulation** is the influence of the target phoneme on surrounding phonemes. This chapter looks at three particular consonants (/ɹ/, /l/, /ŋ/) that are strongly influenced by coarticulation. Although many consonants have unique qualities, these three warrant additional detail as explained here.

THE /ɹ/

The orthographic r, as it is written from language to language, varies more in pronunciation than any other consonant in the IPA. Because of this variation, the IPA devotes seven symbols to it on the consonant chart, rhoticity in the diacritic section, and the open-mid, central, unrounded vowel /ɜ/ in the vowel section.

During the Old English period, the trilled /r/ was used by most speakers. This vowel was carried into Middle English and is still used in British-English. In American-English, according to the IPA (1949), the R with right tail /ɽ/ or the lowercase R (/r/) were used by most speakers. They were transcribed in broad transcription as /r/. According to the IPA (1996), the turned R /ɹ/ is now the accepted GAP pronunciation in the initial position of CV words and in CCV /stɹ/, /skɹ/, and /spɹ/ syllables that are unaspirated.

Variations of the /ɹ/ in CCV Syllables

As mentioned earlier, the r is greatly influenced by coarticulation. The /ɹ/ becomes voiceless in a CCV syllable when preceded by a voiceless stop such as /p/ in pry [pɹaɪ], /t/ in trim [tɹɪm], or /k/ in crow [kɹo] or a voiceless fricative such as /f/ in free [fɹi], /ʃ/ in shrink [ʃɹɪŋk], or /θ/ in thread [θɹɛd]. These are indicated in broad transcription with the /ɹ/ but in narrow transcription the under-ring /ɹ̥/ is added to the /ɹ/ symbol. The /ɹ/ is unchanged in CCV clusters such as /stɹ/ in string [stɹɪŋ], /skɹ/ in scratch [skɹætʃ] and /spɹ/ in spry [spɹaɪ] if the stop is unaspirated, otherwise the /ɹ/ becomes voiceless.

Variations in the /ɹ/ in VC Syllables

According to the phonological rules of the English language, the /ɹ/ can only close syllables containing the vowels are /ɪ/, /ɛ/, /ɑ/, /ɔ/ and the diphthongs /aɪ/ and /aʊ/. When the diphthongs /aɪ/ and /aʊ/ are combined with /ɹ/ there are two pronunciations. The word could be pronounced as a monosyllabic word such as fire [faɪɹ] or a bisyllabic word such as [ˈfaɪ jɚ].

The combination phonemes /ju/ can also be combined with /ɹ/. (It is important to note that the /oʊ/ and the /ɔɪ/ can be in syllables closed by /ɹ/, but most individuals using GAP do not use these pronunciations; Ladefoged, 1993.) In addition, the open-mid, central, unrounded vowel /ɜ/ combined with rhoticity is used in many GAP pronunciations.

The vowel plus /ɹ/ combinations are often referred to as **centering diphthongs.** The centering diphthongs are /ɪɹ, ɛɹ, ɑɹ, ɔɹ, juɹ, aɪɹ, and aʊɹ/. The /juɹ/ is used mostly in more formal speech and is often replaced in everyday speech by the /ɜ/ with rhoticity. The word [pjuɹ] in formal speech becomes [pɝ] in everyday conversation.

The vowels /i/, /e/ can be combined with the /ɹ/ only in multisyllabic words by changing the /ɹ/ to /ɚ/ and placing an intrusive approximant /j/ between the vowel and the r variation. This is also true of the /o/, however, the /w/ is the intrusive approximant. Multisyllabic words are discussed in chapter 8.

Words containing a /d/, /n/, or /æ/ use the fish-hook R (ɾ) in narrow transcription.

Other r Phonemes

/r/: voiced, alveolar trill (LOWER-CASE R)—Spanish.

/ʀ/: voiced, uvular trill (SMALL CAPITAL R)—French.

/ɾ/: voiced, alveolar tap (FISH-HOOK R)—Spanish.

/ɽ/: voiced, retroflex flap (R WITH RIGHT TAIL)—in Nigeria.

/ʁ/: voiced, uvular fricative (INVERTED SMALL CAPITAL R)—French.

/ɻ/: voiced retroflex approximant (TURNED LONG-LEGGED R)—dialects of American-English.

/ɝ/ open-mid, central, unrounded vowel with rhoticity (RIGHT-HOOK REVERSED EPSILON).

/ɚ/: schwa with rhoticity (RIGHT-HOOK SCHWA).

THE /ŋ/

Because of nasal coarticulation and phonological rules, the /ŋ/ can only be combined with the /ɪ/, /ɛ/, /æ/, /ɔ/, /ʌ/, and /ɑ/ vowels in GAP. When pronouncing these vowels followed by the /ŋ/, the vowel may sound different than it would in other contexts due to the influence of nasality. The /ŋ/ is found in medial and final positions.

THE /l/

The /l/ phoneme is the only lateral approximant in GAP and it varies significantly based on its position in the word. In the initial position of a CVC syllable, the voiced lateral approximant /l/ is produced as in light [laɪt]. When the /l/ follows a vowel, precedes another consonant or ends a word, it becomes a velarized /ɫ/ often called a dark l.

When the /l/ is followed by the front vowels /e/ or /æ/, it becomes retracted and is pronounced as /leʊ/ and /læʊ/, respectively. When /l/ is followed by the back vowel, /o/ is often omitted. This is true in words like *pole* [pol]. The /l/ is present only when the speaker is using emphasis and exact pronunciation. Because of their unique character, /l/ words like *sail* are often difficult to transcribe correctly using broad transcription. The correct transcription of the word *sail* using broad transcription would be /sel/.

When vowels /i/, /e/, /u/ and diphthongs /aʊ/, /aɪ/, or /ɔɪ/ are combined with the final /l/, the word can often be pronounced as monosyllabic or bisyllabic, for example, *fail* [fel] or [ˈfe jəl]. The /l/ also becomes syllabic in unstressed syllables in multisyllabic words at the conversation level. (More information on this is available in chapter 9.)

Review Questions

1. What is coarticulation?
2. How many variations of the orthographic r are there in the IPA?
3. What r is used in GAP in the initial position and in unaspirated /stɹ, skɹ, spɹ/ blends?
4. When is r voiceless in CCV syllables?
5. What are the centering diphthongs?
6. What vowels can be combined with the /ŋ/?
7. What l is used in initial position?
8. What is the dark l? When is it used?

Exercises

1. Transcribe the following into phonetics:

/ɪɹ/	/ɛɹ/
deer	air (err)
veer	bear (bare)
leer	care
beard	fare (fair)
clear	hare (hair)
feared	pair (pear)
hear (here)	their (there)
year	scare
sneer	wear (where or ware)
pierce	share

/ɑɹ/	/ɔɹ/
car	bore (boar)
barge	door
mart	lore
heart	war
arm	store
far	core
jar	nor
large	pour (pore)
par	soar
yard	roar

2. Transcribe the following words into phonetics in the monosyllabic form only (is the word monosyllabic, bisyllabic, or both?):

/aɪ/	/aʊ/
lair	hour
fire	flower (flour)
choir	tower
hire	power
tire	sour
dire	scour
wire	
pyre	
spire	
buyer	

3. Transcribe the following /ɝ/ words into phonetics:

fur

jerk

earth

earn

church

work

first

burn

serve

hurt

herd (heard)

4. List five words that can be transcribed using the /juɹ/.

5. Transcribe the following words into orthography noting various spellings:

tʃɝp	dɝt	kɝb
baɹb	tʃaɹm	daɹk
gɪɹ	mɪɹ	nɪɹ
faɹm	aɹth	aɹd
tʃɔɹ	fɔɹs	goɹp
dɛɹ	lɛɹ	mɛɹ
kɔɹk	poɹtʃ	soɹt
ɪɹ	tʃɪɹ	fɪɹs
sɝdʒ	pɝl	aɹ
vɪɹ	bɹɪm	tʃɝʃ

gɝˑl	ɝl	bɝˑθ
ɹɛɹ	tɛɹ	swɛɹ
hɑɹθ	ɔɹz	bɔɹd
glɛɹ		

6. Transcribe the following /ŋ/ words into phonetics noting the vowel:

bang	bong
cling	swing
hung	sung
song	sang
pong	pang

    Think of two more for each of the five vowels.

7. Transcribe the following /l/ words into phonetics (note whether the /l/ is velarized):

lace	loft
led	lie (lye)
lid	lake
load	love
lymph	lean
all	bell
bill (Bill)	null
bale (bail)	sale (sail)
tale (tail)	ail (ale)
kale	Dale (dale)
fail	jail
hail (hale)	mail (male)
nail	pail (pale)

quail	rail
sail (sale)	stale
scale	veil (vale)
whale (wail)	Yale
trail	Braille
frail	flail
Gail (gale)	shale

8. Transcribe the following /l/ words paying close attention to the vowel preceding the /l/:

    seal   sill   sail   sell   Sal   peel   pill   pail   pell   pal

NOTES

Chapter 8

Syllable Stress

Stress is the rhythm of the language. In pronunciation, stress is the word, part of a word, or one word in a group of words that receives the most emphasis. This emphasis is the result of loudness, pitch, length of the syllable, or some combination of the three variables. Understanding and denoting stress appropriately is a difficult concept for most beginning phoneticians and individuals learning ESL. The complexibility of stress is directly related to the variability of pronunciation in the English language.

Stress is not variable in all languages. Like English, the German language uses variable stress patterns. Other languages use fixed-word stress or fixed-phrase stress patterns.

FACTORS INFLUENCING STRESS

In Old English, many words were monosyllabic. If the word was multisyllabic, the first syllable of word was always stressed with the exception of those words beginning with a prefix. If the word began with a prefix the next syllable was automatically stressed. This straightforward and consistent pattern of syllable stress was disrupted when loanwords from various languages entered into Middle and Modern English.

Because there is no governing body to dictate pronunciation, grammar, and spelling rules for the English language, many factors effect stress patterns. These factors include but are not limited to standards of pronunciation, the formality of the speaking situation, and dialects. Each of these factors is discussed in detail in subsequent chapters.

SYLLABLE STRESS

Syllable stress refers to the part of the word that is most prominent. (Syllable stress is referred to by some authorities as **accent.**)

There are two main types of syllable stress recognized by the IPA. The symbols used to denote stress can be found in the suprasegmentals section of the IPA.

At the word level, **primary stress** is denoted by a superior vertical stroke (/ ' /) as in *apple* [ˈæp əl] and **secondary stress** is denoted by an inferior vertical stroke (/ ˌ /) as in *yellow* [ˈjɛ ˌlo]. A syllable receiving either primary or secondary stress is considered to be a **stressed syllable.** There are also syllables that receive no stress. No symbol of any type is placed on a nonstressed syllable; however, only certain vowels can appear in these syllables.

VOWELS IN STRESSED AND UNSTRESSED SYLLABLES AND WORDS

In GAP, the vowels /i, ɪ, e, ɛ, æ, ʌ, u, ʊ, o, ɔ, ɑ/ can appear in a stressed syllable or a stressed word. The /ɝ/ from the other symbols section of the IPA can also appear in a stressed syllable. The /ɪ, ə, ɚ/ can appear in an unstressed syllable. The /ɪ/ is the only vowel that can appear in both stressed and unstressed syllables and words.

Because GAP has a large number of words ending in variations of the y suffix, a narrow transcription symbol has been devised. The use of the understrike raising sign (/̝ /) under the /ɪ/ as in /ɪ̝/ provides an accurate representation of the sound made by the these suffixes. The barred i (/ɨ/) is also used in unstressed syllables to replace the /ɪ/. The /ɨ/ is a close, central, unrounded vowel considered by some authorities to represent the desired pronunciation.

INTRUSION APPROXIMANTS

The approximants /w/ and /j/ are frequently used as intrusives in conversational speech. The intrusive phoneme appears in words such as *buyer* [ˈbaɪ jɚ] or *employee* [ˈɛm ˌplɔɪ jɨ] or between words at the phrase level, as in *how about* [ˈhaʊw əˈbaʊt].

The inclusion of an intrusive approximant (also called **transition glides**) is not always necessary when pronouncing individual words. It is possible for two vowels or a vowel and a diphthong in adjacent positions to be pronounced clearly in slow, formal speech. The use of **open juncture,** which is a short pause between phonemes, syllables, or words, allows for the vowel pronunciation without an intrusive approximant. In conversational speech, **closed juncture,** which is the smooth transition between phoneme, syllables, or words without a time separation, invites the use of intrusive approximants. The student is encouraged to use intrusive approximants at the word level for practice. Occasionally other consonants are used as intrusives.

STRESS PATTERNS

Good listening skills are crucial to mastery of the concept of syllable stress. At the two syllable level, four patterns of stress are commonly used. The understanding of these basic patterns provides an important framework for stress identification. As the words increase in syllable length, fewer set patterns can be identified. In multisyllabic words, the student must learn to hear the variations.

Monosyllabic Words

At the word level, all monosyllabic words are stressed. It is interesting to note that most monosyllabic words come from the Old English and are among the 1,000 most frequently used words in the English language.

Bisyllabic Words

There are four common patterns that can be noted in pronouncing and transcribing two syllable words at the word level.

Type 1

Type 1 is exemplified by two syllable words in which the first syllable receives primary stress and the second syllable receives no stress. In these words the second syllable is usually a syntactic marker added to a one syllable word. (Note the endings are written in phonetics and may have a variety of spellings.) The following are commonly used syntax markers that receive no stress: /əl, ən, ɚ, ɪŋ, nəs, ɪdʒ, ənz, ɪs, ɪʃ, əm, ət, əst, əz, ɨ, fəl, ləs/. The small capital /ɪ/ can be used interchangeably with any schwa symbol. Examples of Type 1 follow:

/əl/ as in [ˈte bəl]
/ən/ as in [ˈɹi zən] or [ˈop ən]
/ɚ/ as in [ˈæk ɚ] or [ˈpe pɚ]
/ɪŋ/ as in [ˈmoɹn ɪŋ] or [ˈstɑp ɪŋ]
/nəs/ as in [ˈkaɪnd nəs]
/ɪdʒ/ as in [ˈkɑl ɪdʒ]
/ənz/ as in [ˈhæp ənz]
/ɪs/ as in [ˈpɹæk tɪs]
/ɪʃ/ as in [ˈɹæd ɪʃ]
/əm/ as in [ˈkɑm ən]
/ət/ as in [ˈbɪs kət]
/əst/ as in [ˈklos əst]
/əz/ as in [ˈtɔs əz]
/ɨ/ as in [ˈbɪ zɨ]
/fəl/ as in [ˈblis fəl]
/ləs/ as in [hop ləs]

Type 2

Type 2 is exemplified by two syllable words in which the first syllable receives no stress and the second receives primary stress. The following prefixes receive no stress according to pronunciation rules carried over from Old English (note the prefixes are written in phonetics and may have a variety of spellings): /ə, bə, kəm, kən, də, dɪs, əks, ɪn, əb, pɹə, ɹə, fɚ, sə, tə, mɪs/.

Although the pronunciation rules clearly indicate no stress should be placed on the first syllable, many individuals place primary stress on a prefix. In these pronunciations, the word follows a Type 3 pattern. Note the alteration of the vowels. Remember the schwa can only appear in an unstressed syllable. Following are Type 2 examples. (Note, the first word follows pronunication rules, whereas the second word reflects another commonly used pronunication pattern explained in Type 3.)

/bə/ as in [bə ˈhaɪnd] or [ˈbi ˌhaɪnd]
/kəm/ as in [kəm ˈplt] or [ˈkʌm ˌplit]

/kən/ as in [kən ˈvɪns] or [ˈkʌn ˌvɪns]

/də/ as in [də ˈfit] or [ˈdi ˌfit]

/dɪs/ as in [dɪs ˈkʌs] or [ˈdɪs ˌkʌs]

/əks/ as in [əks ˈsɛpt] or [ˈɛks ˌsɛpt]

/ɪn/ as in [ɪn ˈsaɪd] or [ˈɪn ˌsaɪd]

/əb/ as in [əb ˈtus] or [ˈɑb ˌtus]

/pɹə/ as in [pɹə ˈtɛnd] or [ˈpri ˌtɛnd]

/ɹɚ/ as in [ɹɚ ˈgɑɹd] or [ˈri ˌgɑɹd]

/fɚ/ as in [fɚ ˈgɪv] or [ˈfɔɹ ˌgɪv]

/sə/ as in [sə ˈpoz] or [ˈsʌ ˌpoz]

/tə/ as in [tə ˈde] or [ˈtu ˌde]

/mɪs/ as in [mɪs ˈtek] or [ˈmɪs ˌtek]

In order to fully understand the variability of pronunication, try pronouncing these words in each of the two ways previously mentioned. These words can also be pronounced a third way by altering the primary and secondary stress on the words such as [ˌtu ˈde].

Type 3

Type 3 is exemplified by one syllable receiving primary stress and the other syllable receiving secondary stress. Although it is more common to have the first syllable receive the primary stress and the second syllable receive the secondary stress, the other variation is often used in pronunication. In either case the vowels used must reflect stressed syllables. Type 3 examples follow:

[ˈjɛ ˌlo] or [ˌjɛ ˈlo]

[ˈvæl ˌju] or [ˌvæl ˈju]

[ˈfɑ ˌlo] or [ˌfɑ ˈlo]

Type 4

Type 4 is exemplified by both syllables receiving primary stress. These words are also called compound words. Examples of Type 4 words follow:

[ˈbes ˈbɔl]

[ˈhɑt ˈdɔg]

Bisyllabic Word Practice

Identify which type of stress pattern you feel you use in your speech and, using this pattern, transcribe the following words into phonetics including syllable stress marks. In order to better understand variations in pronunciation, transcribe the words using different stress patterns where applicable. The words are organized by consonant phonemes. There are 10 bisyllabic words for each consonant phoneme with the target phoneme in the initial position. The consonants are organized in cognate pairs where applicable. In order to practice phonological patterns, label each word after it is transcribed in terms of CVC, and so on. Remember there are no words in GAP that use the /ʒ/ or the /ŋ/ in the initial position.

/p/ and /b/

pagan	babble
pastel	bacon
patrol	beaver
pencil	boa
pigment	boiler
polo	buffet
punish	boxer
peon	bugle
potter	boric
power	billion

/t/ and /d/

table	diet
timber	digit
total	deacon
tanker	debate
toilet	disease
tacky	dual
tepid	dozen
tuna	dumbbell
tussle	double
tower	dipper

/k/ and /g/

cabbage	gable
cackle	gala
cadet	golden
carbon	getting
cola	gory
copy	gumdrop
cunning	gopher
convince	gifted
cupful	ghastly
kinder	goggle

/m/   /n/

(These phonemes are not cognates.)

macaw	gnomish
machine	navy
mental	nickel
motor	noel
movie	neglect
mutton	nightgown
music	nitwit
minute	nothing
moving	nutmeg
mattress	nylon

/f/ and /v/

phony	visor
fizzle	vacant
finish	vaccine
finger	vagus
fatten	value
festive	vestal
foible	vocal
phooey	volley
fungus	volume
fondue	viva

/θ/ and /ð/

thankful	themselves
thousand	thereby
thymus	thyself
thumbnail	therewith
thinner	therefore
thinking	thenceforth
theta	therein
thesis	thereof
thorax	thereon
thorny	thereto

/s/ and /z/

saber	zany
cymbals	zebra
pseudo	zero
sidewalk	zombie
scepter	zonal
selfish	zillion
select	zenith
saying	Zoe
subdue	zipcode
supply	zigzag

/ʃ/   /h/

(These phonemes are not cognates.)

sharper	hamster
shaving	hapless
shoelace	heckle
shoddy	heighten
sharpen	horseback
shipment	humus
sugar	hyphen
shuffle	hungry
chauffer	hymnal
chalet	hydrant

/t ʃ/ and /dʒ/

chamber	gender
channel	gentle
chapter	giant
challenge	jabber
charcoal	
jangle	
chicken	jester
chestnut	jealous
cherub	jungle
chili	junction
chuckle	

/w/   /ʍ/

(These phoneme are not cognates.)

waken	whining
wanly	whimsy
weapon	whisper
within	whereas
water	whitefish
welcome	whistle
witness	whetstone
weasle	whaler
widget	whiten
Waldo	wheedle

/j/

(These phonemes are not cognates.)

/j/	/l/
yeasty	labor
union	lactose
yammer	leaving
yardage	linen
Yankee	locket
yearly	longhorn
yarrow	ledger
yogurt	liar
yucca	lyric
yelper	luncheon

/ɹ/

racial

raffle

railway

restless

robin

rummy

routine

writer

wrestler

wrapper

Multisyllable Words

As you can see from practicing syllable stress at the bisyllabic word level, many stress patterns depend on individual pronunciations. Because speech is dynamic and ever changing, detailed rule study at the multisyllabic word level has limited value. **Practice and listening** are the keys to mastering stress patterns. Remember, multisyllabic words may have more than one syllable that receive secondary stress. Listed here are some sample pronunciation patterns for three and four syllable words. In these patterns primary and secondarily stressed syllables are both labeled stressed. These are included as examples and are in no way indicative of all possible pronunciation patterns.

Sample patterns for three syllable words are as follow:

1. Stressed–unstressed–unstressed: [ˈæn ə məl]
2. Unstressed–stressed–unstressed: [dɪs ˈgres fəl]
3. Unstressed–stressed–stressed: [ʃə ˈkɑ ˌgo]
4. Stressed–unstressed–stressed: [ˈbʌ fə ˌlo]
5. Stressed–stressed–unstressed: [ˌi ˈlɛk trɪk]
6. Stressed–unstressed–stressed: [ˈbæs kət ˌbɔl]

The pattern shown in Example 6 applies only to compound words in which one of the words is more than one syllable. In these cases the following pattern is also acceptable: [ˈbæs kət ˈbɔl]

Sample stress patterns for four syllable words are as follow:

1. Stressed–unstressed–unstressed–unstressed: [ˈkwɛs tʃən ə bəl]
2. Unstressed–stressed–unstressed–unstressed: [dɪs ˈgres fəl lɨ]
3. Unstressed–stressed–stressed–unstressed: [ə ˈkɑm ˌplɪʃ mənt]
4. Stressed–unstressed–stressed–unstressed: [ˌɛr ə ˈmæ trɪk]
5. Stressed–stressed–unstressed–unstressed [ˌo ˈbi sə tɨ]

Syllable Stress Rules

Woods (1990) provided numerous rules pertaining to stressing syllables. These rules are included for information only. Remember, all rules have exceptions.

1. Words ending in ity, ety, ic, ical, ify, efy, ia, ial, eal, ible, ion, ional, ian, ean, ium, ient, ience, iency, inal, ious, eous, uous, graphy, and logy place the primary stress in the syllable immediately before the suffix.
2. Words ending in ate, ous, ent, ence, ency, ant, ance, ancy, ary, ory, tude, graph, and gram place primary stress two syllables before the ending.
3. Words ending in ade, ee, eer, osis, ese, esque, ette, oon, itis, aque, ique, and igue stress the suffix.

Multisyllabic Word Practice

Transcribe the following words into phonetics using stress marks. In order to better understand variations in pronunciation, transcribe each of the words using different stress patterns where applicable. These words are organized by initial position consonant phonemes. The consonants are organized into cognate pairs were applicable. In order to practice phonological patterns, label each word after it is transcribed in terms of CVC, and so on.

/p/ and /b/

Pacific	babysat
paprika	beginner
peppermint	bulletin
pillowcase	bacteria
permissible	biology
patriotic	buttonhole
polysyllabic	bazooka
pacify	buffalo
panacea	beverage
patella	belittle

/t/ and /d/

telecast	daffodil
tuition	deposit
tomato	diminish
typical	dynamic
tobacco	diary
taxpayer	denial
tamale	definite
tapioca	dormitory
timidity	diameter
terminal	diligence

/k/ and /g/

cabinet	governor
colorful	gorilla
colony	gardener
kingfisher	gasoline
comedian	garrison
continental	getaway
camera	guarantee
chemistry	gazebo
convention	gallery
coconut	guesswork

/m/   /n/

(These phonemes are not cognates.)

manager	narcissus
mandolin	negative
microfilm	nectarine
meteor	nominee
mollify	nomadic
motorcar	nursery
mercury	nutrition
mortify	nausea
martial	nemesis
Miami	nutcracker

/f/ and /v/

factory	vanilla
pharmacy	vanity
fanciful	valentine
fiesta	vehicle
foliage	villager
fascinate	vertigo
fugitive	visual
feminist	viaduct
philosophy	vitamin
favorite	violent

/θ/ and /ð/

theorize	thereunder
therapy	therethrough
thirty-two	thereafter
thundering	thereabout
theater	thereinto
thermostat	therein
before	Thanksgiving
theretofore	theology
thematic	thoroughbred

/s/ and /z/

celery	czarina
sanity	zestfully
seaworthy	zeppelin

selection	zodiac
syllable	zinnia
sumptuous	zucchini
several	zonation
settlement	zoology
successor	zygomatic
satellite	zirconium

/ʃ/ and /ʒ/

(There are no /ʒ/ phonemes in the initial position.)

shuffleboard

sharpening

chandelier

Chevrolet

chivalry

shuttering

sugarbush

showmanship

shamelessly

chaperon

/h/

habitat

halibut

holiday

honeybee

holiness

whoever

hummingbird

haphazard

heroic

hermitage

/t ʃ/ and /dʒ/

champion	gelatin
churchgoer	janitor
chokecherry	genuine
checkerboard	jalopy
chinchilla	jettison
chatterbox	jellyfish
chimpanzee	javelin
charitable	jovial
chumminess	germicide
charwoman	juxtapose

/w/   /ʍ/

(These phonemes are not cognates.)

waterfall	whichever
wilderness	wheezingly
wallpaper	whimsical
wolverine	whatsoever
wonderfully	whiffletree

watermelon   whimpering

wearisome   whirlybird

wintergreen   whippoorwill

woodpecker   wherewithal

wiliness   whippersnapper

/j/   ## /l/

(These phonemes are not cognates.)

eulogy   larceny

eureka   lowering

utilize   legacy

usury   leftovers

uvula   luminous

youthfully   limitation

utensil   latitude

unity   lavender

unicorn   ladybug

uniform   laundromat

/ɹ/

recital

rectory

ramshackle

reaction

reluctant

rheumatic

wrongfully

respective

ridicule

romantic

Review Questions

1. Define stress.
2. How is emphasis determined?
3. Is syllable stress variable in English? In other languages?
4. What changed the consistent stress patterns used during Old English?
5. What are the four patterns used in bisyllabic stress patterns? How are they denoted in the IPA?
6. How is an unstressed syllable denoted in the IPA?
7. In GAP, what vowels can appear in unstressed syllables?
8. What is unique about the /ɪ/?
9. What narrow transcription symbol or vowel can be used to denote the suffix y?
10. What is an intrusion approximant? When is it used?
11. What is open juncture? What is a closed juncture?
12. Can other consonants be intrusive in words? Cite an example?
13. Are all monosyllabic words stressed at the word level?
14. What suffixes receive no syllable stress?
15. What prefixes, by rule, receive no syllable stress but in pronunciation may be stressed?
16. What do we usually call words when both syllables receive primary stress?
17. Can a multisyllabic word have more than one secondarily stressed syllable?
18. How can a student master stress patterns at the multisyllabic word level?
19. In labeling stressed and unstressed syllables, are secondarily stressed syllables considered to be stressed?
20. Are the rules pertaining to syllable stress always followed in pronunciation?

Exercises

1. List four common bisyllabic word stress patterns and an example for each written in phonetics with stress denoted.
2. List the common stress patterns for three syllable words and give an example for each written in phonetics with stress denoted. Do the same for four syllable words.
3. Transcribe the following compound words indicating stress as appropriate:

sunset   rainbow

playground   blackboard

airplane   wigwam

daylight	footstool
birthday	cupcake
meatball	highchair
ice cream	dishpan
necktie	hopscotch
bluejay	sunshine
dollhouse	bedroom

4. Transcribe the following words with the target phoneme in the medial and final position. Identify which type of stress pattern you use in your speech and, using this pattern, transcribe the following words into phonetics including syllable stress marks. In order to better understand variations in pronunciation, transcribe the words using different stress patterns where applicable. You will note that the words are organized by consonant phonemes. In order to practice phonological patterns, label each word after it is transcribed in terms of CVC, and so on.

/p/

crockpot	gossip
caper	tulip
papoose	elope
octopus	cityscape
unpopulated	hula hoop
apologize	potato chip
popover	handicap
opposite	censorship
slipping	regroup
trapeze	housetop

/b/

| about | ice cube |
| bobcat | kabob |

robot	cobweb
robin	inscribe
cabinet	ear lobe
labial	describe
tubercular	bathtub
sabotage	spare rib
rubber	imbibe
ribbon	prescribe

/t/

(Note the variation in pronunciation of the medial /t/.)

data	await
heater	jacket
daughter	pollute
guitar	quintet
editor	coconut
litter	omelet
quieter	violet
operator	supermarket
related	underset
theatre	tomcat

/d/

tedious	avid
daddy	batted
hiding	lucrid

strident

radish

vandal

sadden

shadow

federa

cider

salad

rated

myriad

punted

denude

David

alkaloid

/k/

beacon

blocker

bobcat

brackish

sackful

accident

acknowledge

American

handicapped

apricot

clinic

oblique

shellac

slowpoke

artistic

chaotic

republic

piggybank

ladylike

gigantic

/g/

again

baggage

bongo

auger

cognate

jiggle

bedbug

fatigue

prologue

nutmeg

moneybag

polliwog

foggy	washrag
figure	intrigue
kangaroo	eggnog
regalia	handbag

/m/

beaming	alum
camel	income
cement	lifetime
comic	monogram
bambino	truism
diminish	telegram
amulet	diagram
December	realism
reimburse	helium
edema	phoneme

/n/

boner	campaign
finish	beacon
frowning	alone
cannon	define
canoe	fortune
kennel	lion
panic	machine
lanolin	napkin

universe   open

volcano   yeoman

/ŋ/

anger   hiding

jingle   evening

wrangler   finding

finger   morning

kingdom   bullring

lingering   coloring

elongate   buying

kingly   hollering

English   going

swinger   wedding

/f/

afar   aloof

cafe   Joseph

differ   sheriff

golfer   monograph

before   enough

aphid   belief

affix   telegraph

hyphen   cutoff

useful

traffic

rainproof

midriff

/v/

advance

bevy

clever

event

devil

giving

heaven

level

over

weaving

alive

captive

behave

endive

passive

naive

votive

deceive

mangrove

remove

/θ/

author

bathhouse

diphthong

ruthless

withhold

rethink

something

methane

mothy

pithy

beneath

bypass

eyetooth

uncouth

warpath

locksmith

aftermath

twentieth

underneath

broadcloth

/ð/

(There are a limited number of words with /ð/ in the final position.)

bother	unswathe
brethren	enwreathe
brother	unclothe
father	rebathe
clothing	bathing
rather	smoother
weather	seething

/s/

facet	business
fossil	fireplace
glasses	focus
racer	gracious
lasso	tennis
pieces	radius
loosen	lioness
Pacific	toothless
voices	promise
popsicle	police

/z/

bazaar	bases
clumsy	echoes
easy	sunrise
newsprint	pillows

advisor	paralyze
opposite	potatoes
plaza	bananas
pleasant	because
stanza	denies
Susie	arose

/ʃ/

action	cherish
bashful	blackish
earshot	polish
mansion	yellowish
special	undernourish
tissue	embellish
ration	establish
kosher	sunfish
usher	astonish
pressure	relish

/ʒ/

adhesion	garage
aphasia	corsage
confusion	massage
diversion	mirage
leisure	prestige
vision	fusilage
treasure	sabotage

fusion	camouflage
usual	entourage
visual	rouge

/t ʃ/

feature	approach
matches	cockroach
henchman	impeach
hitching	butterscotch
peaches	avalanche
moisture	sandwich
nature	outstretch
picture	ostrich
rancho	bewitch
watchful	hemstitch

/dʒ/

fledgling	divulge
eject	forage
codger	garbage
digit	encourage
drudgery	cartilage
educate	manage
pigeon	vestige
pages	rampage
logic	voyage
legion	porridge

/w/

(There is no final /w/ in GAP.)

always	guesswork
awake	sidewalk
awkward	reword
werewolf	kilowatt
edelweiss	handiwork

/j/

(There is no /j/ in the final position in GAP.)

billion	kayak
lawyer	humor
genius	coyote
value	royalty
junior	minuet

/l/

collie	avail
driller	duel
feelings	parole
elapse	betrayal
toilet	cathedral
villian	windmill
silent	serial(cereal)
colorful	ritual
finale	obsolete

NOTES

Chapter 9

Narrow Transcription and Factors Influencing Pronunciation

This chapter covers the two important theory concepts of **narrow transcription** and **factors influencing pronunciation.** Some of the narrow transcription symbols have been introduced previously, but the following is a comprehensive listing of the symbols commonly used to delineate allophones. (Note that not all narrow transcription symbols are included. Only those symbols commonly used at an introductory level have been listed.)

The second part of this chapter examines syllabic consonants, clusters, abutting consonants, the glottal, and the assimilation of selected consonants.

NARROW TRANSCRIPTION

Narrow transcription is differentiated from broad transcription in the use of allophonic variations denoted by specific symbols. In the IPA narrow transcription symbols are included in the diacritics and suprasegmental sections. Although narrow transcription can be of value in any conversational transcription, it is invaluable to the speech/language clinician when transcribing defective speech or phonological errors. It is also helpful to the phonetician transcribing dialects or pronouncing words from foreign languages.

Commonly Used Diacritics

The following is a listing of commonly used diacritics; an example of each follows the description.

1. The subscript wedge (/ ̬/) indicates partial voicing of a voiceless phoneme: [ˈlɪ t̬əl].
2. The subscript bridge (/ ̪/) indicates the dentalizing of a nondental phoneme: [d̪aɪv].
3. The under-ring (/ ̥/) indicates nonvoicing of a voiced phoneme: [b̥ɹaun].
4. The superscript H (/ʰ/) indicates aspiration: [pʰɑt].
5. The superimposed tilde (/~/) indicates the velarizing of a nonvelar phoneme: [puɫ].
6. The superscript tilde (/ ̃/) indicates nasalization of a nonnasal phoneme: [s̃no].

7. The subscript w (/ ʷ/) indicates labialization of a nonlabial phoneme: [t ʷɔl].
8. The syllabicity mark (/./) indicates a syllabic consonant: [ˈæp̩ l̩].
9. The understrike raising sign (/ˌ/): [ˈtaɪ nɪ̞].

Commonly Used Suprasegmentals

The following is a list of commonly used suprasegmentals.

1. The length mark (/ː/) denotes lengthening of a phoneme.
2. The half-length mark (/ˑ/) denotes partial lengthening of a phoneme.
3. The breve (/˘ /) indicates a shortened phoneme.
4. The under-dot (/. /) indicates a syllable break. (This can also be denoted by a space.)
5. The slash (\) indicates the end of a phrase (breath group).
6. The double slash (\\) indicates the end of a sentence (intonation group).
7. The superior vertical stroke (/ˈ /) indicates primary stress.
8. The inferior vertical stroke (/ˌ/) indicates secondary stress.

Other IPA Symbols Commonly Used

The following are other commonly used IPA symbols.

1. C Cedilla (/ç/) is a voiceless, palatal fricative. It is used by many speakers at the colloquial level to replace the /h/ in words like [çu].
2. The barred I symbol (/ɨ/) is used in unstressed syllables sounding like the /i/.

FACTORS INFLUENCING PRONUNCIATION

Syllabic Consonants

The three syllabic consonants in GAP are the /n̩/, /m̩/, and /l̩/. These syllabic consonants can be used only in the final unstressed syllables and the syllabicity mark appearing under the consonant replaces the unstressed vowel. Syllabic consonants are used in rapid, informal speaking situations.

Transcribe the following words into phonetics using syllabic consonants. Indicate stress as appropriate.

/l̩/	/n̩/
cancel	deacon
expel	chicken
fuel	chosen

royal   dozen

apple   garden

/m̩/

alum

atom

bottom

maxim

random

Clusters

As discussed in chapters 1 and 6, words are formed using a variety of consonant and vowel combinations. Based on these combinations, some words become more difficult to pronounce. When two consonants appear together in transcription they form a cluster or an abutting consonant situation. A cluster is when two consonants of different places of articulation are produced together in the same syllable. When produced, the two articulatory postures are attempted simultaneously, creating a strong first consonant and a shorter duration second consonant with gliding characteristics. Abutting consonants are discussed later in the chapter.

Clusters can appear in the initial, medial, or final positions of words. Initial clusters are usually formed by combining various consonants with the /s/, /ɹ/, or /l/ phonemes. Examples are the words *sleep* [slip] and *grin* [gɹin]. Medial clusters usually appear at the beginning of a second or third syllable in a multisyllabic word. Examples are the words *regrowth* [ˌɹi ˈgɹoθ], *apply* [ə ˈplaɪ], and *askew* [ə ˈsku]. Final position clusters are composed of a variety of phonemes including /sk/ as in *desk* [dɛsk], /mp/ as in *camp* [kæmp], /ns/ as in *mince* [mɪns], /st/ as in *fast* [fæst], and /ŋk/ as in *bank* [beŋk].

Final position clusters are also formed when the past tense marker /t/ is added to a voiceless consonant such as *staffed* [stæft] or the /d/ is added to a voiced consonant such as *bagged* [bægd]. Final position clusters are also formed when the plural marker /s/ is added to a voiceless consonant such as *maps* [mæps] or the /z/ is added to a voiced consonant such as *adds* [ædz]. (Note that some phoneticians consider the /ts/ and /dz/ to be affricates.) When a /ə/ is inserted between the two consonants it is no longer considered a cluster.

In GAP, the orthographic symbol x is considered a cluster written as /ks/ such as *axe* [æks] and the orthographic symbols qu is a cluster written as /kw/ as in *queen* [kwin]. Clusters are often simplified by children whose speech is developing.

Transcribe the following monosyllabic words containing consonant clusters into phonetics indicating stress as appropriate. Indicate the cluster or clusters in each word by underlining them. What consonants are more commonly paired to form clusters? What cluster pairs are formed as the syntax varies?

/p/

plant	plug
please	prank
prom	spell
spot	spoil
spin	priest
crept	script
grips	maps
clamps	thumps
limp	help
pulp	ramp

/b/

blip	blind
blank	brace
brig	broad
broom	blond
bloat	block
rubbed	subbed
cubs	pubs

/t/

state	stock
store	trail
trap	tree
twig	twine

twelve	twin
jerked	stilts
forced	sorts

/d/

dwell	dwarf
drab	drape
dread	drill
drive	drop
drove	drown
combed	clothed
hosed	loaned

/k/

cleft	cling
crib	croup
scant	scout
quake	quill
queen	clean
barked	act
box	six

/g/

glad	glib
globe	grant
grave	grease
Gwen	gleam

grove	gray
plagued	bugged
mugs	hugged

/m/

smack	smug
smile	smoke
smooch	smelt
smith	smash
smooth	small
vamp	bump
champ	primp
brims	dimmed
lymph	film

/n/

snack	snub
snout	snip
snail	snoop
snow	sniff
snatch	snarl
mourn	once
whence	chant
spent	tenth

/ŋ/

brings	gangs

things   gongs

dinged   think

/f/

flub   flag

flame   flies

flex   free

phrase   French

fresh   fry

left   safes

gulf   lymph

/v/

scarve   sweaves

wolves   waves

delve   twelve

love   drevs

/θ/

threw (through)   throng

thrill   thrift

thrive   throne

throb   three

threat   throat

forth   strength

cloths   fifth

/s/

sphere	scout
slug	smoke
sneeze	space
staff	swam
snow	stand
rest	task
whiffs	disk (disc)
sweats	crisp
nix (Nick's)	fierce

/z/

bathes	sends
cones	robes
codes	

/ʃ/

shrank	shred
shrink	shrugs
shrub	shrine
shrill	shriek
shrew	shroud
swooshed	borsch
washed	brushed

/t ʃ/

arched	crouched
March (march)	porch
bunched	broached

/dʒ/

bilged	lounge
gouge	daged
sponge	twinge

/w/

Guam	quartz
quake	quell
swank	sweet
twig	twerp

/l/

blight	block
fleece	flee
glum	globe
clam	clutch
plead	plunk
sleigh	sling
owls	child
self	silk
twelve	bolt

/ɹ/

brag	dress
phrase	grin
crime	prank
trail	thrash
tree	frame

Abutting Consonants

Abutting consonants are two consonants appearing together in transcription but separated by a syllable break. Many possible combinations of abutting consonants are found in GAP. The manner of articulation of the various abutting consonant effects the pronunciation. Words formed by abutting plosives are often difficult to pronounce. Some particular examples are words formed by two different abutting plosives such as *stop gap* ['stɑp 'gap], words formed by the same abutting plosive such as *cat tie* ['kæt 'taɪ], and words formed by two plosives of similar place of articulation such as *hot dog* ['hɑt 'dɔg]. Another difficult pronunciation is when a plosive is followed by a fricative. In this case an affricate is formed such as *hot shot* ['hɑt ʃɑt].

Abutting consonants often yield difficult to pronounce syllable patterns. Because a consonant followed by a vowel is the easiest pattern to produce, it follows that other patterns involving two or more consecutive consonant are more difficult to produce. CVCCC and CCVCCC patterns are among the most difficult patterns to produce. When words are difficult to produce they are often mispronounced.

Transcribe the following commonly mispronounced words into phonetics indicating stress as appropriate. Try using a variety of pronunciations and indicate the problem with the incorrect pronunciation.

February	picture
library	athlete
realtor	mirror
diphthong	asks
naphtha	larynx
temperature	frothed
warmths	strengths
prompts	asps
romped	

The Use of the Glottal

As discussed in chapter 5, the glottal is nonphonemic in GAP. Although it is nonphonemic, it is sometimes used in pronunciation. It is most frequently used in medial position of words ending in the orthographic symbol n such as *kitten* [ˈkɪ ʔən] or to separate two "n"s in words like *counting* [ˈkaʊnʔ ən]. Notice that in the word *counting,* the /ŋ/ is changed to an /n/. The glottal may also be used in other abutting consonant situations containing a /t/ and ending in an unstressed /ən/.

The use of the glottal in these situations is most common in the eastern dialect. GAP generally uses the /t/ (the partially voiced /t̬/) or the /d/ in medial t spellings. The use of the glottal replacement in other situations in GAP is considered a phonological error.

Transcribe the following words into phonetics indicating stress as appropriate and using the glottal where applicable. Try practicing the words using alternate pronunciations.

cotton	Britain
mountain	bitten
batting	fatten
greeting	mitten
netting	rotten
setting	skating

Assimilation

Assimilation is the influence of one phoneme on a neighboring phoneme in a syllable, word, or phrase. Although all phonemes are effected by assimilation, the proximity of certain consonants in a word or phrase may have an increased influence. Some consonants appearing in recurring positions such as *nanny* [ˈnæn ɨ] or *fifty* [ˈfɪftɨ] do not create difficult pronunciations; however, others such as *scissor* [ˈsɪz ɚ] or *lullaby* [ˈlʌl ə ˌbaɪ] are difficult to pronounce. Because the /ɹ/, /l/, and /s/ are considered among the most difficult consonants to pronounce, they are problematic when recurring in the same word or in words near each other in a phrase. When a phrase contains words that make it difficult to pronounce, it is called a **tongue twister.**

Assimilation can also result in a change in manner of articulation of the adjoining consonants. One particular example of this is the /n/ before the /k/ as in *ink* [ɪŋk].

Transcribe the following words with recurrent phonemes into phonetics indicating stress as appropriate.

cease	since
sauce	soapsuds
surface	thesis

incense	assessor
secession	sensitive
landlord	lovely
lulu	loyal
local	lastly
level	lullaby
error	after
restroom	reindeer
rural	rumor
writer	warrior
rupture	nearer

Transcribe the following phrases with recurrent consonants into phonetics. (Note that the individual words loose their identity.)

ill will	six ships sailing
toll call	ripe red roses
roll call	ship ashore

Review Questions

1. How are narrow transcription and broad transcription differentiated?
2. Why would a speech pathologist use narrow transcription?
3. When are the following narrow transcription symbols commonly used?
    a. partial voicing
    b. partial nonvoicing
    c. aspiration
    d. velarization
4. How do we indicate the end of a phrase? How do we indicate the end of a sentence?
5. What is syllable value?
6. What three consonants can become syllables?
7. When are syllabic consonant used?
8. What is a cluster?
9. In what position of words can clusters be found?
10. How are final position clusters related to plurals, past tense, and affricates?
11. What are abutting consonants?

12. List several types of abutting consonants that are difficult to pronounce.
13. When is the glottal commonly used in GAP?
14. What is assimilation?
15. What are some examples of consonants influencing consonants?

Exercises

1. Give several examples of CVCCC and CCVCCC words.
2. Transcribe the following words into phonetics using syllabic consonants. Note stress as appropriate.

fickle	feeble
golden	random
feeble	dabble
dimple	heathen
spasm	dampen
system	stickum
capon	tandem
channel	carton
chuckle	problem
gable	Latin
gentle	listen
parson	parcel
castle	mention
action	million
sandal	seven
tunnel	solemn
waggle	symptom
totem	museum
seven	woman
salon	sharpen

tension	tuition
villian	William
municipal	purple
ample	inedible
reliable	feeble
liable	visible
suitable	sable
cymbal	

3. Transcribe the following words containing both clusters and abutting consonants into phonetics. Note stress as appropriate. After transcribing the word, indicate whether it contains a cluster, abutting consonants, or both.

/p/

Plato	platter
plutonium	player
pretest	presto
premium	spasm
spaghetti	spookier
airplane	exploit
impeach	pamper
April	interpret
employee	duplicate
capsize	upstart
inspect	abrupt
biceps	relapse
caterpillar	

/b/

blackball	blossom
blockbuster	bracelet
brainless	breakup
brimful	bravado
bloodmobile	bluish
amber	lumbar
abloom	problem
library	umbrella
carbon	orbit
verbal	barbaric
absorb	

/t/

staple	static
stuffy	transfer
travel	trivet
tweedle	twitch
twenty	stereo
after	victim
outlook	loyalty
printing	ritzy
statue	matrix
mortal	itself
swiftly	afflict
adult	invent

subscript	duets
chemist	subvert
salutes	talent
unmarked	coerced
inserts	typists
locusts	

/d/

dwindle	dwelling
drafty	drama
drawer	drizzle
dramatic	drinkable
dropsical	druid
laundry	address
sundry	padlock
meddling	boulder
wildcat	garden
bandage	hinder
wizard	tattered
almond	attend
homeland	island
foothold	grandchild
rebuild	upheld

/k/

closet	clapping
cradle	cracker

schedule	skinny
quiver	quota
scruple	squashy
dishcloth	alcove
junky	concrete
orchid	expire
rescue	discuss
cactus	bookworm
describe	object
monarch	chipmunk
apex	larynx
mollusk	unmask
enact	

/g/

glacier	gladden
glassy	gracious
grading	greetings
guana	glucose
glottis	greenbacks
aglow	giggling
igloo	engross
regret	migrate
argue	wigwam
zigzag	neglect

/m/

smarter	smuggling
smorgasbord	smokiest
smattering	smirky
smitten	smithereens
smidgeons	mashup
helmut	schoolmate
pampers	impend
armhole	goldsmith
classmate	revamp
platform	alarm
inform	

/n/

snorkel	snooty
snowball	snappish
sneakers	snuggle
snagging	snazzier
snowmobile	Snoppy
hinder	plunder
inundate	tornado
censor	agency
rancid	fancy
dental	into
background	highland
balance	license

quadrant   vacant

billionth   prevent

tolerance   patients (patience)

/f/

frosty   fraction

freedom   frenzy

frontage   flocking

flabby   flagpole

flaky   flower

afflict   chiefly

elfkin   alfalfa

belfry   refresh

airfield   orphan

asphalt   softness

adrift   hayloft

ingraft   engulf

itself   myself

beliefs   layoffs

tariffs   makeshift

/v/

salvo   solving

velvet   silver

culvert   larva

servant   nervous

harvest   intervention

evolve

ourselves

absolved

themselves

/θ/

thriller

thresher

thrower

throatiest

threefold

filthy

enthrone

monthly

hyacinth

thready

threeply

thruway

thrombosis

thriftier

panther

bathroom

hundredth

millionth

/ð/

farthest

worthier

trustworthy

northerly

seethes

/s/

student

scary

smuggle

speller

Sweden

squadron

asphalt

stinker

sliver

sniffle

stereo

scraggly

sprayer

brisket

axiom	extra
priceless	also
dismiss	glancer
gospel	synopsis
arson	distal
gutsy	upstream
cutoff	sunmask
icebox	impulse
silence	elapse
divorce	florist
buckets	harvests

/z/

bathrobes	yields
exams	salesman
sevens	caves
frenzy	Wednesday
exactly	cobwebs
rids	eczema
bushels	backyards
bedrooms	drawings

/ʃ/

shrapnel	shrimper
shrubberry	shrinking
shrewdly	shrillest

shredded	shriveling
shrinkage	shrunken
airship	censorship
overshoes	membership
overshade	undersheriff
marshall	portion
partial	overshadow

/h/

downhill	yahoo
manhole	
cohort	behavior
beholden	cohesion
dehydrate	inhumane
inhaler	

/t ʃ/

archduke	orchard
scorching	torture
starchy	marching
fortune	parchment
parcheesi	mortuary

/dʒ/

angel	cordial
gingerly	margin
bargeman	barging

scavenging   prodigy

porgy   larger

Margy   orange

lozenge   impinge

arrange   enlargement

prearrange   surcharge

revenge   George

enlarge

/w/

guava   quagmire

quaintly   sweetbread

swivel   swelter

squalor   twisting

twilight   tweedle

linguist   sanquine

aqua   equal

liquid   doorway

disquiet   aqueous

aquatic   frequent

/j/

trillion   valuable

loyalty   humorous

union   continue

unused   senior

monument   stallion

/l/

flapjack	flashing
gluten	glossy
clinker	climate
planner	plumage
sleeveless	slither
babbling	boulder
kindling	elfish
horsefly	eaglet
welcome	prickly
salvo	helmet
houseplant	helping
walrus	marlin
juiceless	pulsate
alto	atlas
involve	drevolves
insults	stealth
difficult	convulse
buttermilk	rectangle
itself	billfold

4. Transcribe the following CCC clusters into phonetics. Note stress as appropriate.

midst	scream
square	next
glimpse	street
screen	squawk

splint	sprig
cysts	wrists
gifts	oinks
sixth	crypts
crisped	blintz
cringed	milked
quilt	scents
fenced	scalped
bunked	prompt
ponds	waltzed
lounged	coins
benched	cinched
square	straight
splatter	squall

5. Transcribe the following r variations and diphthongs in phonetics indicating stress as appropriate.

appear	experience
material	period
nearly	spirit
adhere	frontier
clearly	killdeer
prepared	declare
affair	square
various	very
chairing	despair
compare	staring

welfare	repair
article	gardener
farmer	army
starry	afar
darting	farther
tardy	corner
order	quarter
forest	forward
important	foreign
gory	ashore
downpour	border
during	you're
fury	allure
jury	attire
backfire	desire
empire	inspire
inquire	wired
sattire	sapphire
flyer	coward
astound	roundup
sounding	return
certain	further
journal	purpose
hurry	person
thirty	service

earlier	prayer
mayor	alone
lowered	aisle
pile	lion
byline	silence
reply	finally
society	aloud
about	outside
amount	thousand
allow	flower
annoy	ahoy
decoy	enjoy
destroy	annoint

NOTES

Chapter 10
Sentence Stress

Sentence stress refers to the most prominent words in a phrase or a sentence. English is a stress-timed language (see Fig. 10.1) with a predetermined rhythm. In other words, approximately every 0.6 seconds a stressed syllable must occur (Woods, 1992). These syllables may follow a variety of patterns that affect the length of the stressed and unstressed syllables, but the length of time required to pronounce the various sentences is the same.

English, typically, has a predetermined rhythm, and the syllables seem to scramble to accommodate this beat. The rhythm requires a major stressed syllable every 0.6 seconds, and there are normally one or two unstressed syllables near each major syllable:

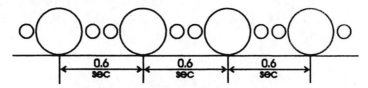

The rhythm of a typical English sentence

The rhythm is maintained by the stressed syllables. If there are several unstressed syllables around the stressed syllable, its duration is shortened, and the unstressed syllables must be glided over very rapidly:

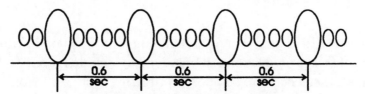

The rhythm with several unstressed syllables

If there are no unstressed syllables nearby, the stressed syllables are naturally lengthened in order to fill the spaces of 0.6 second intervals:

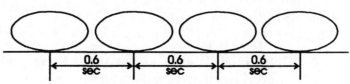

The rhythm with no unstressed syllables

FIG. 10.1. English is a stress-timed language (reproduced with permission of the Minister of Public Works and Government Services Canada, 1997, from *Rhythm and Unstress*; information from Public Service Commission of Canada).

Using Fig. 10.1, note how the following examples fit into the patterns:

Pattern 1: [ðə ˈæn ə məl ˈɪz ə ðə ˈpɔɹtʃ nɚ ðə ˈskɹin dɚ//]
Pattern 2: [ˈtʃɪl dɹɪn ʃəld nət bə əˈlaʊd tə ˌple jə ˌlon ˈnɪɹ ə kən dʒəstd
ˈstɹit//]
Pattern 3: [ˈgo ˈtu ˈbɛd ˈnaʊ//]

CONTENT AND FUNCTION WORDS

Content words in the language are nouns, verbs (including auxiliary verbs, formed with not), adjectives, adverbs, possessive pronouns, and interrogatives. **Function words** (also called **functors**) are prepositions, articles, personal and relative pronouns, possessive adjectives, demonstratives, conjunctions, auxiliary verbs, and the expletive **there.** Function words are responsible for more than 30% of our language (Woods, 1992). Some common function words are *a, am, an, and, are, as, at, but, by, can, could, do, does, for, from, have, I, if, in, it, me, my, of, on, or, she, should, so, than, that, the, their, them, till, to, up, was, we, you.*

FORMALITY OF THE LANGUAGE LEVELS OF PRONUNCIATION

The stress pattern used at the phrase or sentence level is highly interrelated to both the formality of the language and the intonation pattern. (Intonation, the pattern of variation in the pitch of the language, is beyond the scope of this text.)

There are four levels of pronunciation that reflect the formality of the speaking situation: stage speech or public reading style, formal speech or public speaking style, formal colloquial or vernacular, and familiar colloquial or everyday speech. Each of these levels of speech vary in terms of rate of speech, the number of stressed and unstressed words, the situation, the dialect, and vocabulary.

Stage Speech or Public Reading Style

This is the type of speech that is used in a formal presentation situation in which a large group of people are listening. It is used for stage productions, literary readings, church services, or other settings when there is little audience contact. Sentences are composed primarily of stressed words making the pronunciation clear and deliberate. Open juncture and a slow rate of speech are common. The GAP dialect is used and the vocabulary is sophisticated.

Formal Speech or Public Speaking Style

This type of speech is used in group presentations, small group settings, and dyads. Particular situations might include a lawyer presenting in the courtroom or an interviewee answering questions with a prospective employer. This style might also be used when talking to individuals in authority or positions of importance. This style requires exact pronunciation and a precise sophisticated vocabulary. This requires open juncture with many stressed words and a slow, deliberate rate using General American Speech.

Comments on the Stage and Formal Speech

When using stage or formal speech, the speaking rate is about 140 words per minute (**wpm**). This slow rate allows for open juncture and full pronunication of all vowels and consonants. There is little use of the schwa vowel with the exception of adding the schwa to the end of words for emphasis such as [ˈspikə]. All final consonants are pronounced including nt, nd, and other CC endings, the voiceless plosive /p, /t/, and /k/ are aspirated and the /ʍ/ is used in lieu of /w/ for wh spellings. At this level of speech, even function words may be stressed. The monothongs /e/ and /o/ become diphthongs and /ju/ is used in all types of /u/ contexts such as new /nu/ becomes /nju/.

Formal Colloquial or Vernacular

The **vernacular** is the type of speech used in everyday situations involving conversation with people in structured situations. (The term **colloquial** refers to speech in a familiar setting.) These situations vary from a classroom lecture given by a teacher and involving questions and answers from the class, to a conversation with a store clerk during the purchase of a selected item. Rate is about 160 wpm and is less deliberate using fewer stressed words. Regional dialects are used and a variety of appropriate vocabulary. Although technical or occupational terms may be used, slang is not acceptable.

Everyday Speech or Familiar Colloquial

Familiar colloquial speech is used in everyday, casual situations with friends, family, or close acquaintances. The rate of speech is 180 wpm or faster with closed juncture, few stressed words, and less precise pronunciations. The pronunciations are characterized by dropped endings particularly in CC contexts such as nd or nt. Consonant changes such as /n/ for the /ŋ/, /d/ for the /ð/, /t/ for the /θ/, /dʒ/ for the /ʒ/, and /w/ for both wh and w spellings, the voicing of voiceless phonemes such as the /θ/ in the medial and final position. Vocabulary is relaxed and may contain slang type words. Regional dialects are used.

DETERMINING PHRASE AND SENTENCE PATTERNS

Once the level of pronunciation is determined, the content and the type of phrase or sentence can be determined.

Content of the Phrase or Sentence

Consider the following sentence: **"We want a dog."** If the meaning of this sentence can be answered with the question, "Who wants a dog?" it would be stressed as follows: [ˈwi ˌwɑnt ə ˌdɔg//]. If the meaning of the sentence can be answered with the question, "What about a dog?" it would be stressed as follows: [ˌwi ˈwɑnt ə ˌdɔg//]. If the meaning of the sentence can be answered with the question, "What do we want?" it would be stressed as follows: [ˌwi ˌwɑnt ə ˈdɔg//].

Type of Sentence

The stress pattern will vary depending on whether the sentence is a statement, question, command, or exclamation. Also, factors like affirmation or negation are important. Consider the following sentences:

Statement: [ˈɑɪ ˌse ə ˌfɪʃ//]
Question: [ˌdu ˈju ˌwɑnt tə ˈgo//]
Command: [ˈstɑp ˈðæt ˈnɑu//]
Exclamation: [ˈɑɪ ˈwɑn//]

At the phrase or sentence level, stress is denoted using a superior vertical stroke (/ ' /) for primary stress and an inferior vertical stroke (/ , /) for secondary stress. The symbols are placed at the syllable level. The words receiving the most emphasis are stressed using the same patterns used at the word level except entire words may be given secondary stress or no stress. A word that receives either primary or secondary stress is considered to be a stressed word and the vowels must be appropriate. No punctuation or capital letters are used in phonetics. A slash (/) is used at the end of a phrase. A double slash (//)is used at the end of a sentence.

Review Questions

1. What is sentence stress?
2. What is meant by the phrase "English is a stress-timed language"?
3. What is a content word? List 10 examples.
4. What is a function word? List 10 examples.
5. What are the four levels of pronunciation? Outline the key points of each.
6. What does the term vernacular mean?
7. What are stress patterns related to?
8. What are the types of sentences?
9. How is sentence stress denoted?

Exercises

1. Write the following words or phrases in phonetics using each of the four levels of pronunciation:

salt and pepper

the little baby whale

what do you want

fried potatoes

with this ring

thousand

in the garage

2. Transcribe the following two word phrases into phonetics indicating primary and secondary stress as appropriate (these phrases are often pronounced as one word):

submarine chaser	school ground
rubber stamp	language arts
blood pressure	clothes hanger
blue ribbon	White House
public school	Virgin Islands
brussel sprouts	vacuum cleaner
hat check	reclining chair
monkey wrench	Santa Claus
pocket watch	malted milk
real silk	fortune telling
gold mine	Middle East
Donald Duck	kettle drum
rip cord	rhythm band
flash card	flutter kick
fly casting	gun runner
guinea hen	goal keeper
beginner's luck	prescription drug
gift catalog	glass blowing
great grandparent	cracker barrel
question mark	tuning fork

3. Transcribe the following phrases into phonetics and indicate stress as appropriate:

mix and match	salt and pepper
wash and dry	long and short

fat and thin	up and down
kiss and hug	horse and carriage
baby and diaper	hot and cold

4. Transcribe the following noun phrases into phonetics and indicate stress as appropriate:

the red ball	the big cat
a small toy	a purple cow
a pink bag	one orange chair
two little rabbits	a large truck
three green apples	a hot potato

5. Transcribe the following noun–verb phrases into phonetics and indicate stress as appropriate:

The girl jumped.

The cat meowed.

A ball flew.

A leaf dropped.

An elephant tooted.

The mail came.

The wind blew.

The painted dried.

An engine roared.

6. Transcribe the following verb phrases into phonetics and indicate stress as appropriate (these can also be considered commands):

Leap high.

Run slow.

Sit quietly.

Stand still.

Swim fast.
Sing sweetly.
Talk softly.
Breathe deeply.
Cry silently.
Shoot straight.

7. Transcribe the following sentences into phonetics and indicate stress as appropriate:

Does the sky look dark?

Wow, the girls like to swim at the beach.

The boys went to the store and bought a tape deck.

The leaves are falling due to cold weather.

The woman went to the store to buy some new clothes.

The birds went flying south for winter.

The cats were enjoying birds and mice for snacks.

Was the zoo crowded, dirty, and hot?

Did the children enjoyed going to the toy store?

Twelve trees fell to the ground during the ice storm.

NOTES

Chapter 11

Standards of Pronunciation and Dialects

STANDARDS OF PRONUNCIATION

American-English is exemplified by variability and flexibility in pronunciation, grammar, and spelling. Although language purists throughout the centuries have encouraged the establishment of a formal "Academy" modeled after the French, no such governing structure has ever been developed. Americans, historically, value freedom and do not endorse any Standard English such as the "King's English" spoken in Britain. Americans do use a variety of criteria to establish acceptable pronunciations and vocabulary necessary for communication.

Acceptable pronunciation and vocabulary are influenced by educated individuals, media personnel, society's heroes, local influence, dictionary explanations, spelling, and the situation. Each of these factors are discussed here.

Educated Individuals. Classroom teachers, religious leaders, and other educated individuals within a community provide a model for others to emulate.

Media Personnel. National news media personnel provide a consistent model of General American speech. Because these broadcasters serve a national audience, the influence of General American patterns is important.

Society's Heroes. Sports heroes, athletes, movie or pop stars, and political leaders provide role models whom others emulate. A particular figure may turn the pronunciation of a unique phrase into a popular one. The Kennedy family has provided the general population with pronunciations that reflect an eastern dialect.

Influence of the Locale. Communities or areas of a state or region often have a unique pronunciation of a word. This is often most evident in the names of towns, villages, or hamlets. In the Rochester, New York area, the village of *Avon* is pronounced [ˌæˈvɑn] and not [ˈeˌvɑn] as the cosmetic company. Another local preference is the pronunciation of the town name *Chili* [ˈtʃaɪˌlaɪ] versus [ˈtʃɪlɨ], which is a food.

Dictionary Pronunciations.   Many speakers trying to pronounce a new vocabulary word refer to the dictionary for the correct pronunciation. Because pronunciation is so variable, the dictionary pronunciation may be different from the conventional pronunciation. The word *cerebral* [ˈsɛɹ ə bəl] is the correct pronunciation according to the dictionary; however, many educated individuals pronounce it [ˌsə ˈri bɹɪl].

Spelling.   As discussed in chapter 1, the English language does not have a direct sound-to-symbol correspondence; therefore, spelling is not always the best indicator of pronunciation. A speaker learning a new word may attempt to pronounce the word as it is spelled. Some common mistakes include *ballet* [ˈbæl ˌe] being pronounced as [ˈbæl ˌɛt].

Type of Situation.   The type of situation refers to the number of participants in the conversation, size of the room, familiarity of the audience, and the importance of the message.

Some Group-Related Pronunciation Standards

Folkspeech refers to the speech of a isolated rural group of people.
Jargon refers to a technical or private vocabulary used for trade or by a professional group.
Street talk refers to a type of speech use by a selected group of individuals. Some examples are:

Homeboy: friend who is a boy in the neighborhood or school

Homegirl: friend who is a girl in the neighborhood or school

Fat: good, fresh, nice looking

Tag name: a name other than your given name by which people refer to you; a nickname

Hood: neighborhood

Water: cops

Afrocops: Black cops

Lime: a casual gathering of friends (used in Trinidad)

ENGLISH AS A SECOND LANGUAGE

Many individuals in the United States are bilingual and use English as a second language. Because American-English has some unique characteristics including a lack of sound-to-symbol correspondence, varied stress patterns and phonemes not used in other language, nonnative English speakers are challenged when learning to pronounce words.

Some of the common pronunciation problems mentioned through the text include the substitution of the /t/ for the /θ/, /d/ for the /ð/, confusions between the /v/ and /w/, and /l/ and /ɹ/. Vowel problems in the form of lack of differentiation of tense and lax vowels also occurs.

DIALECTS

Dialects are best described as speech and language patterns used by a group of people in a geographic location. Dialects reflect subtle differences in pronunciation, vocabulary, and speech rate. They originated due to geographic isolation and historical influences. In the grand scheme of things, American-English is actually a dialect of English. There are other dialects of English including British-English, Australian-English, and South African-English. Historically, American-English began when the 13 original colonies were formed in the 1600s. American-English is a direct outgrowth of Early Modern English as it was spoken in the 1600s in England. The purpose in this chapter is to study the principle dialects of American-English. It is important for all individuals studying dialect to reserve value judgment. Because dialectal patterns result in speech and language differences, it important to remember that no particular dialect is right or wrong. The standard dialect of the American-English is General American. There is much uniformity in the speech of Americans today. This uniformity is the result of the availability of travel, mass media, and better educational systems. This in no way insinuates that eastern, southern, or African-American dialects are inferior.

Historical Background

As discussed in Appendix B, Old English consisted of four main dialects: Northumbrian, spoken in the Northern part of Britain; Mercian, spoken in the Midlands; Kentish, spoken in the Southeast; and West Saxon, spoken in the Southwest. These dialects developed due to geographic location, local leadership, and historical influence. The most influential dialect was West Saxon. This dialect emerged as the standard when King Alfred unified England. Because West Saxon was the official dialect most records are found in this dialect. "Beowulf," the epic poem, is a classic example of this dialectal pattern. Although there are many characteristics of this dialect, one of the most significant was the diphthongization of numerous vowels.

Although the West Saxon dialect was the standard of the time, modern-day English is felt to be a direct descendant of the Angeln dialect.

The Angeln dialect is a combination of the Mercian dialect with some minor influence of the Northumbrian dialect. This dialect is characterized by pure vowels.

As Middle English developed, the Midland dialect became the standard. This can be noted in Chaucer's works. This dialectal growth was closely associated with the movement of the government to Westminister and the growth of London. The Northumbrian dialect split into Northern English and Scottish dialects due to political differences. The Mercian dialect split into west and east sections due to the fact that the East Midlands were ruled by Danelaw and the West Midlands were ruled by King Alfred. The southeastern dialect is a descendant from the Kentish dialect and the southern dialect from the West Saxon.

Modern English was influenced by the continued growth of London, the regrowth of the English language and the great vowel shift. One particular dialect did not emerge during the early modern period, instead a greater London English, which was a combination of East Midland and southeastern, dialects began to develop. The pattern was characterized by various pronunciations of one word and class dialects existing side by side. It was at this time that received pronunciation developed as the standard in England.

American Dialects

The **isoglosses,** or dividing lines, between dialectal regions are never exact and authorities never agree on lines of demarcation. Dialect areas are by their nature overlapping, intertwined, and effected by mobility. The main dialect areas in the United States are New England (eastern), midland (General American) and southern (see Table 11.1 for comparisons of the three dialect regions). African-American dialect is also spoken throughout the United States.

New England (Eastern) Dialect

The New England or eastern dialect is spoken in Maine, New Hampshire, Rhode Island, parts of Massachusetts, Vermont, New York, and New Jersey. This dialect developed from immigrants arriving from the south of England. This dialectal pattern was a direct descendant of greater London dialect. Many of the immigrants were well educated and left England to seek religious freedom.

TABLE 11.1

Comparisons of the Three Major Dialect Regions of the United States

General American	Eastern	Southern
/εɪ/ [tʃεɪ] [skεɪd]	/εə/ [tʃεə] [skεəd]	/e:/ [tʃe:] [ske:d]

When in the final position or preceding a consonant.

General American	Eastern	Southern
/εɹ/ ['kε ɹɨ]	/æɹ/ ['kæ ɹɨ]	/eɹ/ ['ke ɹɨ]

When in the intervocalic (medial position between two vowels) position or beginning a syllable.

General American	Eastern	Southern
/ɪɹ/ [jɪɹ]	/ɪə/ [jɪə]	/ɪ:/ [jɪ:]
/uɹ/ [ʃuɹ]	/uə/ [ʃuə]	/u:/ [ʃu:]

This form is used in more formal communication.

General American	Eastern	Southern
/ɝ/ [ʃɝ] or [ɝn]	/ɜ:/ [ʃɜ:] or [ɜ:n]	/ɜ:/ [ʃɜ:] or [ɜ:n]

This form is more casual and used in colloquial speech.

General American	Eastern	Southern
/ɔɹ/ [hɔɹs]	/oə/ [hoəs]	/o:/ [ho:s]
/aɪɹ/ [taɪɹ]	/aɪə/ [taɪə]	/ɑ:/ [tɑ:]
/au/ [flauɹ]	/auə/ [flauə]	/ɑ:/ [flɑ:]
/ɑɹ/ [stɑɹ]	/a:/ [sta:]	/ɑ:/ [stɑ:]
/ɑ/ [ɑn]	/a/ [an] or /ɒ/ [ɒn]	/ɔ/ [ɔn]

This form is used in all monosyllabic word except those arrested by the /l/.

General American	Eastern	Southern
/ɑ/ [dɑl]	/ɔ/ [dɔl]	/ɑ/ [dɑl]

Those monosyllabic words with the /l/ in final position follow the above pattern.

General American	Eastern	Southern
/ə/ ['bæs kət]	/ə/ ['bæs kət]	/ɪ/ ['bæs kɪt]

This form is used in bisyllabic words.

General American	Eastern	Southern
/ε/ [bεn]	/ε/ [bεn] or /æ/ [bæn]	/ɪ/ [bɪn]

This form is used in monosyllabic words.

General American	Eastern	Southern
/ju/ [fju]	/u:/ [fu:]	/ju/ [fju]

Articulatory Characteristics That Differentiate Eastern Dialect From GAP. The first characteristic differentiating eastern dialect from GAP is the omission of /ɹ/ in all contexts except the initial position. The /ɹ/ is used in the initial position of words such as *red* [ɹεd] or syllables such as *around* [ə'raund] and in initial position CC contexts such as *broom* [bɹum]. Because each word in our language has a time boundary, the omission of the /ɹ/ must be replaced in order to maintain the word timing. The /ɹ/ is replaced with a schwa in all situations such as poor [poə] except following the /a/ vowel as in star [sta:]. After the /a/ the vowel is lengthened as in the southern dialect.

The primary vowel differences between eastern dialect and GAP are the use of /a/ in *apple* ['ap əl] (open, front, unrounded vowel) in the Boston area and the use of /ɒ/ *coffee* ['kɒ fɨ] (open, back, rounded vowel) in short words. The /u:/ is used in place of /ju/ or /ɪu./

In the eastern dialect, /ɜ/ is used for the /ɝ/ and /ə/ for /ɚ/. Finally, eastern speech has more assimilation than General American English and uses a more rapid rate.

Southern Dialect

Southern dialect is spoken primarily in the "deep South" states that border either the Atlantic Ocean or the Gulf of Mexico. These states include North Carolina, South Carolina, Georgia, Florida, Alabama, Mississippi, and Louisiana. This dialect is also spoken in parts of Kentucky, Tennessee, Missouri, Arkansas, Texas, Ohio, Indiana, Illinois, and Maryland. Like the eastern dialect, the southern dialect is a direct descendant of the greater London dialect of the 1600s. The settlers in the southern part of the United States established a "plantation economy." The first settlers who settled in Virginia were quickly followed by others who settled in the area that is now the southern states. All the settlers were seeking land.

Southern dialect has some similarities to eastern dialect. The main difference was that the southern area consisted of hundreds of isolated areas. This isolation caused speech patterns to remain unchanged. The 1700s brought the influence of the slaves and southern Louisiana was influenced by the Arcadians (Cajuns) of Canada.

Articulatory Characteristics That Differentiate Southern Dialect From GAP.

Similar to the eastern dialect, the chief consonantal characteristic is the omission of the /ɹ/ in all contexts except the initial position of CV or CCV contexts. Because the time boundary is affect by the omission of the phoneme, the vowel prior to the omitted /ɹ/ is lengthened. Other r variations include using /ɜ:/ to replace the /ɝ/, the /ə/ for the /ɚ/, /o:/ for the /ɔɹ/, and /e:/ for the /ɛɹ/.

Vowel differences include the use of the /ɔ/ for the /ɑ/, /aɪ/ for both the /aɪ/ and /aʊ/ diphthongs, the use of the /ɪ/ for the schwa in most unaccented syllables not involving rhoticity particularly at the bisyllable level, and the use of /ɪ/ for /ɛ/ at the monosyllabic level.

The southern drawl that characterizes southern dialect is not the result of a slower rate but an increase in pitch range and the diphthongization of numerous vowels. The addition of the /j/ or /w/ approximants followed by a schwa is frequently found in monosyllabic words. This creates the perception of a slower rate.

Finally, the southern dialect uses less nasality than General American English .

Vocabulary Changes Among the Dialects

Each dialectal area has certain words that are used to describe a particular item or event. The origin of these words are historical but the perpetuation of their use is a learned behavior. The following are some examples.

General American	Eastern	Southern
bucket	pail	bucket
seeds	pits	seeds
pizza	pie	pizza
sack	bag	sack
take sick	get sick	take sick
pop	soda	soda pop
[ˈi ðɚ]	[ˈaɪ ðɚ]	[ˈi ðɚ]

African-American English

AAE dialect is considered the fourth major dialect spoken in the United States. It is located throughout the United States and is not **geographically bound**. Although AAE varies from area to area, it has similarities throughout the United States. Some of the characteristics are /t/ for /θ/ in the initial position, /f/ for /θ/ in medial and final positions, and the /d/ for the /ð/ in all positions and the deletion of final consonants. This deletion includes grammatical suffixes and a different use of the verb to be. A nasalized vowel is often substituted for a final nasal consonant such as [mæn] becomes [mæ̃e] (see Owens, 1996, for additional information on AAE).

Regionalisms

Because dialectal areas are large and the lines of demarcation are often unclear, regionalisms often develop. A **regionalism** is a pattern of speech or language particular to a small geographic area. Numerous regionalisms are found with a dialect. Detailed discussion of these various regionalisms is too expansive for this introductory text, but several well-known regionalisms are mentioned.

Boston

The Boston regionalism has received national attention mainly because of the high visibility of the Kennedy family. This pattern of speech is used in the greater Boston area. Most of its characteristics are eastern with the exception of the use of the open, back, unrounded vowel /ɑ/ instead of the near-open, front, unrounded vowel /æ/ used in the General American dialect or the open, front, unrounded vowel /a/ used by the eastern dialect. The use of this /ɑ/ is often considered sophisticated.

New York City

The greater New York City area has one of the largest populations in the world. Through Ellis Island, this area has been a haven for immigrants. One of the important characteristics of this regionalism is its variation. Most of its characteristics are eastern with the following variations: the use of /ɔə/ for /ɔ/, the use of /ɑɹ/ for or spellings, /ɔŋ/ becomes /ɑŋ/, /ŋ/ becomes /ŋg/, /ɝ/ becomes /ʌɹ/, the glottal /ʔ/ is used to replace medial /t/ and /d/ is used for the /ð/ in all level of pronunciation.

Review Questions

1. Is there an "Academy" governing the rules of American-English?
2. List seven factors that influence pronunciation and briefly describe.
3. What is folkspeech?
4. What is jargon?
5. What is street talk?
6. List several common ESL errors.
7. What is a dialect?

8. What do dialects reflect?
9. Is one dialect superior to another?
10. Why is there so much uniformity in American-English?
11. What is an isoglossus?
12. What does the term geographically bound mean?
13. List the characteristics of AAE.
14. Define regionalism.
15. What are the key characteristics of Boston and New York City regionalism?

Exercises

1. List 10 jargon terms used by a speech pathologist.
2. List five words or phrases used in street talk.
3. Make a chart of the dialect areas. Be sure to include name, location, and articulatory characteristics.
4. List 10 vocabulary words or phrases that reflect the dialect areas.
5. Transcribe the following phrases into phonetics using all three dialects:

care for the bear

Marry, Mary, and Jeremy

appear or disappear

the poor horse

a flat tire

a high tower

start the car

Pay a dollar for that salad.

I've been furious.

on the farm

NOTES

Appendix A

Background of the English Language

The study and understanding of the English language is significant to the world as a whole. There are currently 330 million native speakers in 44 countries where English is the official language. This equates to 1.6 billion people or one third of the world's population. This number is in comparison to 260 million people speaking Spanish and 100 million speaking French.

REASONS FOR THE POPULARITY AND PROMINENCE OF THE ENGLISH LANGUAGE

The first reason for the popularity of the English language is its extensive vocabulary base. There are 615,000 current entries in the *Oxford English Dictionary.* This number is significant, also, for what it does not represent. There are an additional 200,000 technical and scientific terms not represented in the dictionary.

Second, English uses a flexible word order, meaning the positions of words can be changed within the sentence. In English it is possible to say "The man drove the car" and "The car was driven by the man." Many words can also act as more than one part of speech. In these examples, the two versions of drive are verbs, however, drive is a noun in this sentence: "Let's go for a drive."

Third, English is actually less complex in its spelling than other languages. Fourth, English uses few tonal variations that effect vocabulary. Fifth, English is relatively gender free. Also, English verbs never have more than five forms and most typically have three. This is in contrast with Latin, which may have up to 120 forms of a verb.

Seventh, spoken English is constantly changing. According to *The New York Times* (1989), it is estimated that 15,000 to 20,000 words per year are added to the language. These words take several forms. Some words are new to the language, like the word *nylon,* whereas others reflect additional meanings of a word such as *bug.* Combinations of previously existing words with new meanings are also introduced, such as *car jacking.*

Finally, the English language is receptive and adaptable to words from other languages. English has not been a pure language since the 5th or 6th century (Bryson, 1991).

WHERE DO WORDS COME FROM?

Words come to the English language as loanwords from other languages. They are created by written mistakes. In the 1934 *Merriam-Webster International Dictionary*, the word *buttonhold* was written by mistake as *buttonhole*. Words are created to reflect new information, a phenomenon, or to attract attention to themselves or the concept they represent. Recent newly created words are *yuppie, gung ho,* and *hype*.

Words change in their meaning. The word *bug* has historically been used to describe an insect. Currently, *bug* is a common expression used to mean an eavesdropping device. (**Fossil expression** is another term for an idiom.) An idiom develops where the original meaning of a word or a phrase changes. An example is a *nitpicker. Nitpicker* literally means ones who picks nits (lice eggs). The idiom means one who is overly concerned about details or one who looks for trivial errors.

Words are created by changing the prefixes or suffixes. The word *cat* can become *catlike* meaning like a cat. Words are incorporated into the language that originally represented a trade name. Some examples include *kleenex*, which is a synonym for facial tissue, and *xeroxing*, which is a synonym for copying.

Finally, words come to the language as alterations of their original form. Some examples are:

Combination words such as *schoolteacher* and *basketball.*
Shortening words such as *pianoforte* to *piano* and *examination* to *exam.*
Words from a group of initials such as *radar* (radio detecting and ranging) and *snafu* (situation normal—all fucked up).
Truncating and joining several words such as *brunch* (breakfast and lunch) or *smog* (smoke and fog).

WHY DO WE STUDY THE HISTORY OF THE ENGLISH LANGUAGE?

Understanding the English language with its variations and idiosyncrasies is crucial to the study of the IPA. The history of the language is not only fascinating, it also provides us with a background for understanding pronunciation, spelling, meaning, and grammatical aspects of the language. It is important to note that linguistic history is deeply effected by current events and key historical events.

Early History of the English Language

It is not known when the first words were spoken or the reasons these words were used. It is believed that man has been communicating using speech and language for about 100,000 years. The first recorded indications of speech were found in the cave drawings in Lascaux, France. These pictograms suggest the presence of a sophisticated lifestyle that undoubtedly included speech and language.

Archaeologists have found the remains of two species named Homo sapiens neanderthalensis (Neanderthals)and Homo sapiens (Cro-Magnons). The **Neanderthal man,** whose existence is dated to 30,000 to 150,000 years ago, was discovered in 1857 in the Neander Valley of Germany. His large brain, short, stocky frame, and course features indicate a less efficient functioning individual. It is believed that these beings lived communally, wore clothes, and used tools. Through the study of fossils, it is believed that Neanderthal man was capable of producing imprecise consonants and vowels. Fine motor control was undoubtedly limited and velopharyngeal functioning nonexistent.

Cro-Magnon man, whose appearance is similar to that of man today, was believed to have come into existence about 30,000 years ago. Archaeologists have found that the larynx of the Cro-Magnon man was deeper in the throat than that of the Neanderthal man. This anatomical change enhanced the capabilities for speech. It is not known whether the laryngeal change was evolutionary or developmental, or even if the Neanderthals and Cro-Magnons were separate species.

The language spoken by the Cro-Magnon was **Euskara**. It is interesting to note that this language is still spoken by the Basques, a small, obscure group of people found in parts of Spain and France. Euskara is believed to be the last remaining neolithic language. Whether all language are "**Global cognates**" or members of the same family is not known, however, there is no known connection between Euraska and any current language.

The Roots of the English Language

There are currently an estimated 2,700 known languages. Languages have evolved over the centuries but common threads can often be identified from language to language. The English language has its roots in the Indo-European group. Essentially, all languages in Europe and the Americas, with the exception of Basque, Estonian, Finnish, Lappish, Hungarian, Turkish, and Native American languages, have evolved from this common group.

Language classifications are based on features such as phonology, morphology, and a descent from a common ancestor. The **Proto-Indo-European** (**PIE**) languages can be traced back as far as 4000 B.C. The original language probably started in Poland or Lithuania and through migration spread across a significant geographic area. PIE is the forerunner of the Indo-European language group as we know it today. The evidence of cognate words that are similar in various languages from different branches of the Indo-European language supports this common ancestry hypothesis. Indo-European is the language group used by peoples who at one time lived in the area of Europe to India, North and South America, Australia and Africa. English is a branch of Low Germanic (Peters, 1968).

The Early Celtic People

The land that is now Great Britain was probably inhabited during the Stone, Bronze, and Iron Ages by the Celtics. It is believed that these people were living in the area when Britain was conquered by Julius Caesar in 55 B.C. (This date represents the beginning of the recorded history of the English language.) The Roman troops did not stay in Great Britain after this invasion, but returned in 43 A.D. and stayed for 400 years. The Celts were part of the Roman Empire called Britannia by the Romans from 43 A.D. to 410 A.D. The Celts' lifestyle was in keeping with that of other countries in the Roman Empire. They were highly civilized; had an effective form of government; and a lifestyle that included amenities such as running water, sanitation, and central heating. Little is known about this period of time. When the Roman Legions withdrew in the early 400s, it is believed that many Celts were absorbed by the Anglo-Saxon tribes. It is also likely that some fled the area and others were killed. Linguistically, all that remains of this early Celtic time frame is a few geographic names.

Early Germanic Tribes

In about 450 A.D., four tribes (Angles, Frisians, Saxons, and Jutes) from the mainland entered what is now Great Britain. The Angles were from Angeln, which is in the corner of Germany. The Frisians were from Holland and western Germany. The Saxons and the Jutes were from northern Europe.

When the Roman legions left Britannia, the Celts fell prey to marauding Picts from the north (what is now Scotland) and Scots from the west (what is now Ireland). The Britons, unable to defend themselves, appealed to the Germanic sea-raiders for assistance.

Little accurate information is available about these tribes. Why did they leave the mainland? Did the tribes work together? Why did the Angle and Jute tribes disappear on the mainland? It is known that the Saxons were the most dominant tribe, but the name England came from Angeln.

The paucity of records is due primarily to the fact that these tribes were functionally illiterate. The history was written in the 731, about 300 years later by a monk named Venerable Bede. His work, entitled *History of the English Church and People,* describes the early history of England, but due to posthumous nature of this history is considered limited in accuracy. The *Anglo-Saxon Chronicles* started by King Alfred also provide information.

The Anglo-Saxons, as the four tribes became known, spoke a similar Germanic dialect that came to be referred to as ɛnɜlisc in the late 9th century upon the request of King Alfred. ɛnɜlisc used a basic alphabet called the Runic alphabet. This is a series of inscriptions marked on a ceremonial stone called a rune.

Christianity

In 597 A.D., St. Augustine brought 40 missionaries to Great Britain. Christianity spread quickly and literacy followed. With the influence of literacy, the language changed to include Anglo-Saxon, Greek, and the Latin influences. (Latin was the language of Christianity. Latin is an outgrowth of the Greek language). Latin alone added more than 400 words to the language during this time period.

Review Questions

1. How many native speakers of English are there in the world today? How many countries use English as an official language?
2. List eight reasons why English is popular as a language.
3. List seven ways in which words come into the English language.
4. Why is the history of the language important to the study of phonetics?
5. How long has man been using speech and language to communicate?
6. Who were the first people to settle Britain?
7. What were the four tribes that influenced England beginning in 450 A.D?
8. What is the significance of St. Augustine bringing Christianity to England in the late 500s.
9. Define the following:

fossil expression   Neanderthal man
Cro-Magnon man   Euskara
PIE   cognate words

Exercises

1. List 10 words that have at least two different meanings (example: *fly*).
2. List five words that you feel are new to the language (or their meaning is new) and five technical or scientific terms. Check the *Oxford English Dictionary* to see if they are listed.

NOTES

Appendix B

Old English (Enȝlisć)

The Anglo-Saxons and Celts used Old English from approximately 449 A.D. to 1100 A.D. The term **Anglo-Saxon** was originally used by 17th-century scholars to refer to the language, but was replaced by modern scholars with the term **Old English**.

In the 5th and 6th centuries, the spoken language sounded very similar to the speech and language of the Germanic tribes. The grammar of Old English was highly inflected and word order was strikingly different than that of Modern English. The true emergence of Old English occurred sometime between the 6th and 9th centuries and was escorted in by the first Germanic consonant shift.

Old English was written in two main scripts. In the early years, the Runic alphabet was used. This was replaced by the Insular script, which was derived from the Irish and Latin beginnings in the early 8th century. It is at this time in history that the use of the Runic alphabet ended. The only sounds that were retained from the Runic alphabet were the /þ/ thorn, /Ᵽ/ wynn and /æ/ ash.

THE FIRST GERMANIC CONSONANT SHIFT

The consonant variations were first systematically explained by Grimm (1822). The following is a summary of these variations.

1. The PIE voiceless stops /p/, /t/, and /k/ became /f/, /θ/, and /h/ (pronounced /χ/)

Latin pedem to *foot*
Latin piscis to *fish*
Latin tres to *three*
Greek kardia to *heart*
Latin centrum to *hundred*

2. The PIE voice stops /b/, /d/, and /g/ became /p/, /t/, and /k/

Latin labium to *lip*
Latin edō to *eat*

Latin duo to *two*
Latin genus to *kin*
Latin ager to *acre*

3. The PIE voiced aspirated stops /bh/, /dh/, and /gh/ became /b/, /d/, and /g/

Sanskirt bhrātɑr to *brother*
Sanskirt rudhiras to *red*
PIE ghostis to *guest*

In summary, /bh dh gh/ to /b d g/ to /p t k/ to /f θ h/.

Additional consonantal changes were also summarized by Verner (1876).

1. Sometimes /t/ became /ð/ in the medial and final positions of words.
2. /p t k s/ became /f θ h s/ in stressed syllable and /v ð z/ in unstressed syllable. (Note the symbols used represent the phonetic sounds not the graphemes used. The /θ/ and /k/ graphemes were not used until Middle English.)

RUNIC ALPHABET

The Runic alphabet was brought to England from the mainland countries by the Germanic tribes. The letters of the alphabet, called **runes,** were a series of strokes originally used for inscriptions, decoration, or to claim ownership. These symbols were carved or etched into objects or on tablets of stone. Each character in the alphabet was actually a word. The (wynn) meant joy or happiness.

The Runic alphabet is also referred to as the **futhorc** (futhark). This name comes from the first six characters, feoh (meaning wealth), ur (aurochs), th (thorn), os (month), rad (riding), and cen (torch). This alphabet was used for about five centuries. It was used concurrently with the other scripts. The thorn was from the Runic. The /æ/ ash and the /ð/ eth from the Latin. It is interesting to note that the word *rune* in Old English means secret or ceremonial stones.

INSULAR SCRIPT

Beginning in the 5th century, after the conversion of Ireland to Christianity by St. Patrick, the half-uncial script was used. This script was a lowercase (minuscule) script. The letters were round but not linked together. In the early 7th century, the monks from Irish monasteries introduced this script to the Anglo-Saxons. The Anglo-Saxons modified this script and developed the Insular script. This script gradually replaced the Runic alphabet.

Old English Symbol Breakdown

Old English, as written by the Anglo-Saxon scribes, used graphemes from several alphabets. The wynn and the thorn symbols were from the Runic, whereas the yogh, eth, and ash symbols were from the Latin. It is believed that all other symbols were from the Irish-Latin (Roman) alphabet. These symbols are actually different from those used today. The following are a close approximation of the symbols ɑ, æ b, c, d, e, f, ʒ, h, i, l, m, n, o, p, r, ʃ, t, ,ð, u, x, y. The thorn and the ð eth were used interchangably in given contexts. The symbols k and z were rarely used. There was no use of j, q, or q. The /χ/ (chi) represented the ks, the c represented the /k/ and /t ʃ/ phonemes. The č was also used for the /t ʃ/ phoneme. The g was represented by the /ʒ/ (yogh) and the /ɣ/ (gamma; a voiced velar fricative.) The /ʃ/ (yogh) was also used to represent the /j/ glide. The macron was used for a long vowel. The wynn was used for the uu or w and the long s /ʃ/ for the s. When double consonants appeared in words they were pronounced twice as a point of emphasis such as cuppe [kʌppə].

It is important to remember that the symbols used in Old English were handwritten using crude instruments on a variety of surfaces. This led to considerable inconsistencies in the Old English phonemes. During the later periods of Old English, the g came into use instead of the yogh in some dialects. Note the use of the a symbol, which is the script a. It was not for many years that the a symbol appeared. Numerous publications erroneously use the two interchangeably.

Consonants

The Stop Phonemes

The stops were p, t, c, b, d, and ʒ. Examples follow:

p as in panne (*pan*)
t as in tid (*time* or *date*)
c as in folc (*folk*)
b as in bread (*bread*)
d as in drincan (*drink*)

ʒ (yogh) had two allophones—ʒ (yogh) as in ʒon (go) and /ɣ/ gamma (a voiced velar fricative) between two vowels as in boɣa (bow). The ʒ (yogh) was also used between two vowels as in beʒen (both). The ʒ yogh, also spelled, jogh had a more rounded top section than that the fricative used by the IPA today in a word like [plɛʒɚ] *pleasure*.

The Fricative Phonemes

The fricatives were f, or ð, h, ʃ, sc. The f had two allophones—/f/ as in fæstan (to make firm) and /v/ as in livas (*lives*). Lives is also written as lifas in some manuscripts.

The Þ (thorn) and the ð (eth) were used interchangeably in all positions in early Old English. In later years, the (thorn) was used in all position but the ð (eth) was used more frequently between two vowels in medial and final positions.

(thorn) in unor (*thunder*) is voiceless.
(thorn) in æt (*that*) is voiced.
ð (eth) in bliðe (*merry*) is voiced.

The h had two allophones—/h/ as in hus (*house*) and /χ/ (chi) as in niχt (*night*). /χ/ is a guttural sound that later replaced the gh spelling. *Night* is also written as niht in some interpretations.

The ʃ had two allophones—/ʃ/ as in ʃand (*send a message*) and /z/ as in nozu (*nose*). The /z/ was sometimes used between two vowels but nosu is also written. The /z/ was frequently used in biblical names. The long /ʃ/ was used in Old English but was pronounced as /s/. sċ as in sċip (*ship*) was pronounced as /ʃ/. The dot is not always used over the /sc/ symbol.

The Affricates Phonemes

The affricates were ċ and cg. ċ as in ceowɑn (*chew*) was pronounced /tʃ/. The dot is not always used over the c symbol. cg as in ecg (*edge*) was pronounced /dʒ/.

The Nasals Phonemes

The nasals were m and n: m as in mægester (*master*). The /n/ had two allophones, both of which were written as n but the pronunciation was different: n as in norð (*north*) and ŋ as in drincɑn (*drink*).

The Lateral Phoneme

The lateral was l: l as in leoht (*light*).

The Trill Phoneme

The trill phoneme was ṙ:ṙ as in ṙæs (*running*).

The Glide Phonemes

The glides were wynn and y as in indɑn (*wind*) and y as in yfel (*evil*). The y was also written as g: geɑr meaning *year*. In the Runic alphabet, /g/ was a glide not a plosive. The /w/ does appear in later Old English.

Consonant Clusters

The following consonant clusters were characteristic of Old English:

/ʒn/ as in ʒnætt (*gnat*).
/hl/ as in hlāf (*loaf*).
/hn/ as in hnoll (*crown of the head*).
/hṙ as in hṙæd (*swift*).
/cn/ as in cnɑwɑn (*know*)
/wl/ as in wlisp (*lisp*).
/wr/ as in wrist (*wrist*).

Both consonants were pronounced in Old English. The /gn/ as in *gnat, gnaw,* and *gnome* [næt, gnɔ, nom], /kn/ as in *know* and *knight* [no, naɪt], and /wɹ/ as in *wrong* and *write* [ɹɔŋ, ɹaɪt] are still used today in spelling but not in pronunciation.

Vowels

Old English vowels were organized into long and short varieties. They were delineated by tongue height, position in the mouth (front or back), and rounding. The symbols for the long and short vowels are exactly the same. The difference is the presence of the macron delineating the long sound. In Tables B.1 through B.4, the vowel in parenthesis is the pronunciation according to the 1996 version of the IPA.

Pronunciation, Tenses, and Suprasegmentals

Little is known about the actual pronunciation of Old English because acoustic records are not available. Through the understanding and study of Latin, however, some information has been gleaned.

It is believed that Old English was phonetic in pronunciation and did not use silent graphemes. Stress was placed on the first syllable of most words. When a prefix was added to a noun, the stress remained on the first syllable, with the exception of the prefixes ge, be, and for. When a prefix was added to a verb, the stress was shifted to the second syllable.

Morphological aspects of Old English show it to be a fully inflectional language with three or four case endings for nouns and adjectives. The use of two tenses, the past and the present, was an outgrowth of the Germanic influence. Auxillaries and compound tenses could be used along with the verbs to enhance meaning. Strong and weak verbs were used. The strong verbs changed vowels as the tense changed and the weak verbs used a /t/ or /d/ at the end to denote tense change but a free word order existed.

Old English scholars believe that the language was fluid when spoken. The reason for the apparent lack of fluidity in written Old English comes from the fact that the early speakers of Old English were illiterate. Although it is believed that the Anglo-Saxon people became literate in the 6th century, it was the scholars and priests who used the Irish-Latin (Roman) alphabet that preserved the manuscripts available today.

Dialects

Old English actually consisted of four main dialect areas. These dialects were perpetuated by geographic isolation, local leadership, and historical influences. These dialects were northern (Northumbrian), midland (Mercian), southeastern (Kentish), and southwestern (West Saxon). Little is known about the northern, midland, and southeastern dialects during Old English. The Southwestern, which became the most influential dialect in the late 9th century, was the dialect of King Alfred.

Scandinavian Influence on Old English

The English were invaded by the Danes and the Norwegians (called the Danes) in 787–794 A.D. and 834–878 A.D. The eastern and northern parts of England were ruled by the Danes for a number of years. The area called Danelaw was recaptured by King Alfred the Great sometime between 849 and 899 A.D. At this time, King Alfred became the overlord of England.

TABLE B.1

Short Vowels

	Front Unrounded	Rounded	Back Unrounded
High	i (ɪ)	y (ü)	u (ʊ)
Mid	e (ɛ)		o (ɔ)
Low	æ (æ)		ɑ (ɑ)

Examples

i as in hinder (below) pronounced [hɪn dɚ]

e as in melu (meal) pronounced [mɛ lʊ]

æ as in cæppe (cap) pronounced [kæp pɛ]

y as in byrd (birth) pronounced [büɹ̈d]

u as in munuc (monk) pronounced [mü nük]

o as in gesod (boiling) pronounced [gɛ sɔd]

ɑ as in sɑcc (sack) pronounced [sɑk]

TABLE B.2

Long Vowels

	Front Unrounded	Rounded	Back Unrounded
High	ī (i:)	ȳ (ü:)	ū (u:)
Mid	ē (ɛ:)		ō (ɔ:)
Low	ǣ (æ:)		ā (ɑ:)

Examples

ī as in sīcɑn (sigh) pronounced [si: kɑn]

ē as in tēon (pull) pronounced [tɛ: jɑn]

ǣ as in tǣsɑn (tease) pronounced [tæ̃ zɑn]

ȳ as in mȳse (table) pronounced [mü: zɛ]

ū as in hūs (house) pronounced [hu: s]

ō as in gōd (good) pronounced [gɔ: d]

ā as in āf (active) pronounced [ɑ: f]

TABLE B.3

Short Diphthongs

ie (ɪɛ) as in sieltan (salt) pronounced [si jəlt]

eo (ɛɔ) as in ceole (throat) pronounced [kɛ jɔ lɛ]

æɑ (æɑ) as in wearm (warm) pronounced [wæ jɑɹm]

TABLE B.4

Long Diphthongs

īe (i:ɛ) as in hīere (safe) pronounced [hi: jɛɹɛ]

ēo (ɛ:ɔ) as in wēod (weed) pronounced [wɛ: jɔd]

ǣɑ (æ:ɑ) as in cēap (price) pronounced [kæ: jɑp]

The English were again invaded by the Danes and ruled by Cnut, Harold Harefott, and Harthacnut for 26 years from 1016 to 1042 A.D. This ended when Edward the Confessor was restored to the throne in 1042 A.D.

It is believed that the Danes spoke a language called Anglo-Norse. Because both Anglo-Norse and Anglo-Saxon (English) were descendants of the same Germanic language, communication was not a problem. Several thousand loanwords from this era are still evident the English language (see Appendix E).

Old English's Impact on Present Day English

Of the 1,000 most frequently used words today in the English language, about 83% are of Old English origin. About 30% of all words used today are directly from the Old English. Some examples of these words are *ale* from alu, *beer* from beor, *book* from boc, *heaven* from heofon, *south* from sunth, *west* from wespero, *winter* from wintra, *summer* from sumor, *win* from gewinn, and *weird* from wyrd.

Literature During the Old English Time Period

Literature from the Old English time period is well preserved and takes the form of both prose and poetry. The greatest poem of this time period is the " Beowulf." This 3,000-line folk epic provides insight into the social conditions, motives, and lifestyles of the time period. The exact author of this particular classic work is unknown, however, information is available on some of the other great writers of this time.

Bede's *Ecclesiastical History of the English People* outlined the history of England. **Alfred the Great** (871–899), an Anglo-Saxon king, was a brilliant statesman, military leader, and prose writer. He started the *Anglo-Saxon Chronicles,* which was a history of important events. These Chronicles continued for more than two centuries after his death. King Alfred is considered the founder of English Prose. **AElfric**, a Benedictine monk and the abbot of Eynsham, is considered the greatest prose writer of the period. The prose and poetry reflected Christian, pagan themes, and historical themes. Many of the great writers wrote in both Latin and the vernacular (English; for more information on Old English, see Peters, 1968).

Review Questions

1. When was the first time the term **Anglo-Saxon** was used?
2. When did Old English emerge?
3. Explain the first Germanic consonant shift. Give several examples.
4. What is the Runic alphabet? Give several examples.
5. What is Insular script? Give several examples.
6. Old English has elements from what two alphabets?
7. Were the double and cluster consonants pronounced in Old English?
8. What is a script A /ɑ/ versus the printed a?
9. What is the difference between long and short vowels?
10. Since there are no acoustic records of Old English, how have scholars learned to pronounce it?
11. Was Old English an inflectional language?
12. How many dialects were used in Old English? What was the most influential one? Why?
13. What are the dates of the Scandanavian influence?
14. What percentage of Old English words are still used today?

15. What is the name of the greatest poem of the Old English period?
16. Name three important prose writers of this time period.

Exercises

1. Write the symbols for the wynn, yogh, eth, ash, thorn, gamma , and the chi.
2. Write each of the consonants, vowels, and diphthongs by category and give an example of each.
3. Copy the symbols from the Runic alphabet and Insular script.
4. Using an Old English dictionary, find five words that have not changed (or have had only minor changes) since Old English times and five words that are no longer used.
5. Review a scholarly work written in Old English. Note the presence of the Old English symbols.
6. List the Old English symbols that we no longer use in orthography but that are used in GAP.
7. List five surnames or geographic locations that use Old English clusters no longer used in the vocabulary.
8. Transcribe the following Old English words into phonetics:

man	wife
child	brother
house	live
fight	drank
eat	sleep

9. Transcribe the following words into phonetics (these words from Scandinavian origin entered the language during Old English):

both	peace
root	loan
skin	weak
law	bathe
wrong	joy

NOTES

Appendix C

Middle English (Englysshe)

Middle English is believed to have started after the Norman Invasion of England in 1066 A.D. and it lasted until the invention of the printing press by Gutenberg in 1454 A.D. Middle English is characterized by extensive vocabulary and grammatical changes, loss of phonetic spelling, and a general decline of the importance of English as a language.

VOCABULARY CHANGES

Beginning with the Norman Conquest in 1066 A.D. and lasting for the next 300 years, French was the official language of the country. Anglo-French (the language spoken by the French who invaded England) was used in the royal court; by the government including the parliament, schools; and in all legal situations. During this time, hundreds of new vocabulary words were introduced and absorbed from the French into the English language.

Numerous Latin words also entered the English language during Middle English. The scholars and educated individuals commonly wrote in Latin words and interspersed English words. Over time, these words became part of the English language.

Forty percent of all French words came into the English language during this time. More than 10,000 loanwords were assimilated. Of these, more than 75% are still in use. Remember, Old English did not have French or Latin loanwords.

GRAMMATICAL CHANGES

The grammar of Middle English changed reflecting **leveled inflections** or weakened inflections (this was the result of Anglo-Norse influence), an added word order, and the new use of prepositions and phrases. Most of the irregular verbs used today are the result of declensions no longer used (*feet, geese, men*).

LOSS OF PHOENTIC SPELLING

Spelling was drastically changed during the Middle English period. During this time period, before the invention of the printing press, books were hand copied by French scholars who did not know the English language. Because of their lack of knowledge, these scholars often introduced their own language. Other factors influencing the spelling variation included the dialectal variations, inconsistent spellings of the same word, and the use of Latin for all learned work.

RESURGENCE OF ENGLISH AND THE RISE OF THE MIDDLE CLASS

The use of Anglo-French was prominent for about two centuries, until English, which had been consistently spoken by the lower and middle classes, became the official language again in 1356-1362 A.D. By the end of Middle English in 1450 A.D., a standardized version of English was used in all legal documents. The growth of London and the movement of the government to Westminister in the 16th century also supported the importance of the English language.

The resurgence of English was also fostered by the Hundred Year War (1337-1453 A.D.) and the Black Death (1349-1350 A.D.). The war helped associate the French language with the enemy and the Black Death killed 30% of the population. This population decrease made the labor class and its language more important.

INFLUENCE OF PROSE AND POETRY

Geoffrey **Chaucer,** using English, became the court poet and through his position exerted influence on the royal family. His use of the vernacular (London dialect) helped with the acceptance of English as an important language.

Middle English Symbol Breakdown

Middle English is actually made up of four different dialects: northern, east midland, west midland, and southern. The east midland was considered the most influential of all the dialects. This was used in London, the university towns of Oxford and Cambridge, and in Westminister, which was the seat of the government. The information presented on the symbol system and changes from Old English to Middle English reflects that east midland dialect is taken from this dialect.

CONSONANTS

Stops

The stops were p, t, k, b, d, and g. Examples of these stops follow:

    p as in pαrαdeios (*paradise*)
    t as in tαlαnton (*talent*)
    k as in kyng (*king*)
    b as in bæddel (*bad*)
    d as in drαgun (*dragon*)
    g as in goute (*gout*)

Changes From Old English

Changes from Old English included using the k instead of the c in most words from Old English. The c, as in corfu (*curfew*), was retained and used in French loanwords. The ʒ yogh was replaced by the g. Finally, the two allophones of the ʒ yogh (the ʒ yogh and the ɣ gamma) were dropped.

Fricatives

The fricatives were f, v, h, s, z, and sh. Some examples are the f as in felowes (*fellow*), the v as in vermelyon (*vermillion*), and the thorn as in [oþer] (*other*). The ð eth was still considered an allophonic variation; however, it was used less frequently in Middle English. (Note the y was also used in late Middle English to replace the initial voiced th sound. This gave rise to phrases like *Ye Olde* meaning *The Old*.) The h had two allophones: h as in hers (*hearse*) and χ chi as in nyχ (*night*). *Night* was also written as nyht in some interpretations. Other examples are the s as in satysfye (*satisfy*), z as in zel (*zeal*), and sh as in shall (*shall*).

Changes From Old English

Changes from Old English included the f and v becoming two distinct phonemes. The v was also written as u. The ð eth became an allophonic variation of the thorn. The y gradually replace the use of the ð eth. By the end of the Middle English period, the th digraph was used. The χ chi became the gh by the end of the Middle English period. The use of the ʃ long s was eliminated. The s was used in words of Old English origin, whereas the c, as in certayne (*certain*), was used for some French loanwords. The s and z became two distinct phonemes, both of which were used to represent voicing. Finally, the sh digraph was introduced instead of sċ.

Affricates

The affricates were ch and dg, j or g. Examples of the affricates are ch as in whyche (*which*), dg as in ledgan (*legend*), j as in joye or ioye (*joy*), and g as in gentil (*noble*).

Changes from Old English

Changes from the Old Enlsih included the c becoming the ch, the cg becoming dg or j or g.

Nasals

The nasals were m and n. An example of a nasal is m as in mocquer (*mock*). The n had two allophones: n as in noble (*noble*) and ŋ as in englysshe (*English*). The ŋ allophone was used when an n preceded a g or a k.

Lateral

The lateral was l, as in lytyl (*little*).

Trill

The trill was the r as in rude (*rude*).

Changes From Old English

There were no changes from Old English to Middle English in the nasals and the lateral. The trill r was written without the umlaut.

Glides

The glides were w and y or g or ʒ. Examples of glides are w as in wyth (*with*), y as in yer (*year*), g as in ger (*year*), and ʒ as in ʒer (*year*)

Changes From Old English

Changes in glides from Old English include replacing the wynn with the w; the j sound was replaced with the y, g, and ʒ; and the ɣ gamma became a w.

Consonant Clusters

Consonant clusters are the loss of h in hl, hn, and hr clusters, the loss of l in wl clusters, and the hw becoming wh or w.

VOWELS

Middle English vowels were organized into long and short vowels. The vowels were delineated by tongue height and position in the mouth (front or back). As in Old English the use of the macron indicates whether a vowel is long or short. In Tables C.1 and C.2, the vowel in parenthesis is the pronunciation according to the 196 version of the IPA.

TABLE C.1

Short Vowels

	Front	Central	Back
High	i (ɪ)		u (ʊ)
Mid	e (ɛ)		o (ɔ)
		a, e, o, y, (ə)	
Low		ɑ (a)	

TABLE C.2

Long Vowels

	Front	Central	Back
High	ī or ȳ (iː)		ū, ōū, ōw̄ (uː)
Mid	ē, ēē, īē (eː)		ō, ōō, (oː)
	ē, ēē, ēā (ɛː)		ǫ, ǫǫ, ǫ̈ų̈ (ɔː)
Low		ā (aː)	

Changes From Old English

Short Vowels. Short vowel changes from Old English include the i (ɪ), e (ɛ), u (ʊ), and o (ɔ) remaining the same. The æ (æ) moved from a low front vowel and ɑ (ɑ) moved from a low back vowel to low central ɑ (a). The two vowels from Old English became one vowel in Middle English. The y (ü) moved from a high, front rounded vowel to a high back unrounded vowel u (ʊ). Finally, the ɑ (a), e (ɛ), o (ɔ), and u (uː) in unstressed syllables were pronounced as a schwa.

Long Vowels. In long vowels, the ī (iː), ē (eː), and ū (uː) remained the same. The ǣ (æː), a low front vowel, became one of two mid front vowels: ē (eː) or ę̄ (ɛː). The ȳ (uː), a high rounded front vowel, became a high unrounded back vowel: ū (uː). The ō (oː) a mid back vowel, became one of two mid back vowels: ō (oː) or ǫ (ɔː). Finally, the ā (aː), a lower back vowel, became a mid vowel.

DIPHTHONGS

Diphthongs from Old English were reduced to single vowels during the Middle English period. Some examples follow:

Old English	Middle English
ie (ɪɛ)	i (ɪ) or e (ɛ)
eo (ɛɔ)	e (ɛ)
æɑ (æɑ)	ɑ (ɛ)
īe (iːɛ)	ē (ɛː)
ēo (eːɔ)	ē (ɛː)
ǣɑ (æːɑ)	ē (eː) or ę̄ (ɛː)

At the same time as this reduction occurred, the emergence of five new diphthongs occurred. These were as follow:

ey /ɑy (áɪ) as in day (*day*) or wey (*way*)
ɑu/ɑw (áʊ) as in cause (*cause*) or drawen (*draw*)
iw/ew (ɪʊ) as in niwe (*new*) or dew (*dew*)
ou/ow (óʊ) as in soule (*soul*) or knowe (*know*)
oi (óɪ) as in chois (*choice*)

OTHER KEY CHANGES FROM OLD ENGLISH

Some of the other key changes from Old English include the cw as in cwen (*queen*) becoming qu as in queen (queen) and ū (uː) as in hūs (*house*) becoming ou (ɔʊ) as in house (*house*). Also, gu was used in some French loanwords in order to clarify words with similar meanings, for example, guard (*guard*) versus gard (*yard*). The plural form en was replaced by the s. The u and v were used interchangeably. *You* was introduced along with other personal pronouns to replace thou, and so on. Finally, /ȯ/ was introduced to prevent confusion of u near stroke letters like m, n, and w, for example, sunu (*son*) became sȯne (*son*). (For more information on Middle English, see Peters, 1968.)

Review Questions

1. What historical events signaled the beginning and end of Middle English?
2. What languages exerted significant influence on the English language during the Middle English time frame?
3. What does the term level inflections mean?
4. Why was spelling so inconsistent during Middle English?
5. What two historical events influenced the resurgence of the English language?
6. What year did English again become the official language of Britain?
7. What great poet influenced the acceptance of English as a language?
8. What are the four dialects?
9. What was the most influential dialect?
10. When was the ŋ allophone used?
11. What changes occurred in the glide sounds?
12. What clusters were lost or modified?
13. What were the new diphthongs?
14. How was the plural formed in Middle English?
15. What sounds were represented by more than one grapheme?

Exercises

1. Outline the changes that occurred in the stop, fricative, and affricate sounds. What symbols were lost?
2. Outline the changes that occurred in the vowels sounds.
3. Using a Middle English dictionary, find five words that have not changed (or have had minor changes) since Middle English times and five words that are no longer used.
4. Review a scholarly work written in Middle English. Note the presence of Middle English symbols.
5. Transcribe the following words of Latin origin into phonetics (these words entered the language during Middle English):

wine   street

pave   mile

wall   school

hymn   disk

pound   exit

6. Transcribe the following words of French origin into phonetics (these words entered the language during Middle English):

tort   noise

coy   rent

soup   fry

roast   stew

broil   judge

NOTES

Appendix D

The Modern Period

The modern period is often divided into two time periods: the early Modern Period that lasted from 1500 to 1700 A.D. and the late Modern Period which started in 1700 A.D. and is still in effect today.

The early Modern Period was escorted in by the invention of the printing press and was influenced by the increased availability of printed materials and books. The Renaissance, the Reformation, and the growth of London as a cultural center also influenced language changes. The early Modern Period saw many changes in pronunciation while spellings became relatively fixed by the use of printing. The spellings used today are symbolic and have been fixed since the beginning of this time period. During this period, Germanic influences faded and grammar became more analytic than inflected.

The late Modern Period, which began in 1700 A.D., was characterized by the attempts to catalog the language into useable, complete dictionaries, the issues of spelling reform, and the continued growth of vocabulary.

THE ROLE OF THE PRINTING PRESS

The invention of the printing press is credited to Gutenberg of Germany in 1450 A.D. It was Caxton, however, who brought printing to England in 1475. The first book printed in English, entitled *The Recuyell of the Historyes of Troyes* (*History of Troy*), marked the beginnings of change in the written word. Spelling standardization was achieved by about 1650 A.D. using the dialect of greater London, which was considered the most important. Because books were far cheaper than manuscripts,they became available to the general population for the first time. By the year 1500 A.D. there were 34,000 books titles printed in Latin and by the year 1640 A.D. there were 2,000 book titles printed in English.

PRONUNCIATION CHANGES

The pronunciation information discussed is based on the dialect of greater London. This was considered the most important dialect by scholars. It is important to note that graphemes, pronunciations, and spelling in this time period were very similar to those used today.

Some significant changes include the following:

1. ʃ was used as a variation of s.
2. j and v began to represent consonants and i and u vowels.
3. The þ thorn and the ð eth of Middle English were used interchangeably and both represented the voiceless sound. The ð eth became voiced in early Modern English and the θ theta became the voiceless sound. Thus, the th became two phonemes instead of one phoneme with two allophones. During the early Modern Period, the use of the digraph th was introduced and widely accepted. These phonemes can be phonemically contrasted in the words *thigh* and *thy*.
4. In Middle English, the n was one phoneme with two allophones. In early Modern English the /n/ and the /ŋ/ became two separate phonemes. Middle English ng became /ŋ/.
5. The use of the /ʒ/ yogh to represent a fricative sound emerged used in French loanwords such as ['liʒɚ].
6. The allophone χ chi of h was lost to English. In many words the pronunciation reflects the dropping of the sound. Examples include [tɔt] and [naɪt]. This was a subphonemic change.
7. In Middle English, the r was trilled in all positions. In early Modern English, the trill was dropped in initial position to equal r and in a centering diphthong to a fricative version /ɹ/.
8. The loss of the pronunciation of the g sound in gn, the w sound in wr and the k sound in kn spellings.
9. The /hw/ phoneme was lost to either /w/ as in [wʊt] or /h/ as in [hu].

GREAT VOWEL SHIFT

Sometime between 1400 A.D. and 1700 A.D. the language experienced a change in the pronunciation of vowels. This is often referred to as the great vowel shift. It was characterized by significant changes in the vowel nuclei from Middle to Modern English. The tongue height for each of the Middle English vowels was raised and the position of the mouth was more restricted. The effects of great vowel shift lasted for many years and during this time numerous pronunciations were used.

In both Old English and Middle English, long and short vowels occurred with clear distinction. This clear distinction was lost in Modern English. Long and short vowels are now written using the same graphemes. It is important to note that many vowels still have allophonic variations that are long and short.

Summary of Changes

The vowel listed in the following represents the spelling used in Middle English and an example of one spelling used in Modern English. The vowel in parenthesis represents the pronunciation according to the 1989 version of the IPA.

Middle English	**Modern English**
ī (i:)	ɑi (aɪ)
ē (e:)	eɑ, ee (i)
ę̄ (ɛ:)	eɑ,ɑ (e) now its (i)

ā (ā)   ɑ (e)
ǭ (ɔ:)   o (o)
ō (o:)   oo, u (u)
ū (u:)   ow, ou (aʊ)
u (ʊ)   u, ɑ (ʌ)
o (ɔ)   o, ɑ (ɒ or ɑ)
ɑ (a)   ɑ (æ)
                               (ɪ, ə) in unaccented syllables

VOCABULARY

Vocabulary continued to grow in the modern period. The early Modern Period saw the regrowth of Classical Greek, with continued Latin and French influence. The expansion of the British Empire lead to the introduction of 50 other languages. Words for the first time came from Italian, Spanish, Portuguese, Gaelic, Russian, Arab, Sanskirt, Chinese, and other languages. Vocabulary was increased by technology, railroads, factories, horsepower, photography, and chemistry. Slang was introduced for the first time.

The Regrowth of English

The regrowth of English is directly influenced by four factors: the Reformation, the Renaissance, the growth of London, and the printing press. The Reformation helped establish English as the language of the learned. This growth of English was accompanied by a nationalism and the continued rise of the middle class after the Black Death. The Renaissance fueled the revival of interest in antiquity, arts, religion, Greeks/Romans, anatomy, communication, and the spread of education. This lead to scientific investigation and scholarly thinking. The growth of London in the late 16th century due to its intermediate position geographically, the location of the great universities of Oxford and Cambridge and a population increase established it as a center for learning. Finally, the printing press brought books and reading to the middle class.

SHAKESPEARE

Shakespeare's importance to the growth in importance of the English language cannot be understated. It is felt that Shakespeare himself possessed one of the largest vocabularies of any English writer. His large vocabulary reflected both his unique use of words and his liberal incorporation of loanwords. His gift to the English language was to increase the acceptable vocabulary and introduce new expressions.

Shakespeare was also instrumental in the accepted use of new pronouns.

The Late Modern Period and American English

The late Modern period existed from 1700 A.D. to the present. Early in this time period, England colonized countries in all parts of the world. Each of these areas gradually developed variations in their speech. The British academy did attempt to regulate language but failed. With colonization it was meaningless to discuss "Standard English."

As the American colonies became settled minor changes began to occur in pronunciation particularly with the r. The American colonies also developed many new vocabulary words and expressions.

Review Questions

1. What historical event marked the beginning of Modern English?
2. What other historical happenings influenced the development of Modern English?
3. Who brought printing to England?
4. How was spelling standardization helped by the printing press?
5. By 1640 how many titles were printed in English?
6. What was a variation of s?
7. What two graphemes became consonants?
8. What digraph was used to represent th?
9. The yogh became what sound? What type of loanwords is it used in?
10. What allophone of h was lost to English?
11. What were the two main allophones of r?
12. What happened to tongue position during the great vowel shift?
13. From which countries did loanwords appear for the first time during the Modern English period?
14. When did slang develop?
15. What is the importance of Shakespeare on the English language?

Exercises

1. Consider the gn, kn, and wr clusters. List five words that begin with each and transcribe into phonetics.
2. List 10 words that use the wh spelling at the beginning. Transcribe each word into phonetics. How many start with /w/ and how many /h/?
3. List other spellings that are used for each of the Modern English vowels listed in the chapter.
4. List five slang phrases. Can you explain their meaning?

NOTES

Appendix E

Alphabets, Writing, Spelling, and Dictionaries Throughout the Years

The understanding of the history of the alphabet, writing variations, spelling changes, and the growth of dictionaries played an integral part in the development of the language. This appendix discusses the historical aspects and how these have influenced the language spoken and written today.

ALPHABETS

Semitic Alphabet

The alphabet used today has a long and varied history. Although the exact origin is unknown, it is believed to be an outgrowth of the **Proto-Semitic alphabet,** whose origins can be traced to what is now the modern Lebanon area. The North Semitic alphabet is most frequently associated with the Phoenicians. Current thinking does not hold that the Phoenicians invented the alphabet, but it is believed that being from a seafaring country the Phoenicians were responsible for spreading it throughout the region. The alphabet used by the Phoenicians has 22 characters but no vowels. Because the Greek, Hebrew, and Arabic alphabets are outgrowths of the Semitic alphabet, many of the 22 characters are still in use today.

It is interesting to note that letters have been organized into a form for thousands of years. Why this form was used is unknown, but speculated reasons include sound of the name, meaning, form, and so on.

Greek Alphabet

Early in the 9th century, the Greeks learned and modified the North Semitic alphabet. Although various local versions of the Greek alphabet were used for about 400 years, the **Ionic alphabet** of Miletos was adopted by Athens in 403 B.C. The Greek alphabet consisted of 19 letters adopted without variation from the Semitic alphabet, however, some of the symbols were changed to become vowels, and several symbols were added, totaling 24 characters. The Greek alphabet is considered by many scholars to be the first true alphabet because it included vowels.

Early Greek writing had an abrupt appearance characterized by short, straight strokes made by a stylus on a wax surface. These abrupt strokes were necessary to avoid wax build up. As the materials used for writing changed, a more curved style of letters appeared. The Greek alphabet also introduced left to right directionality.

Latin Alphabet

The Etuscans learned the Greek alphabet from the Greeks in the 9th century B.C. The Etuscans settled in Rome in 800 B.C. and proceeded to develop a dynasty in the area of the Italian peninsula that lasted 300 years. In 700 B.C., the Romans began using the Greek alphabet in Latin writing. It is believed that Greek and Latin actually developed in the same time period.

The Romans used 21 of the characters from the Greek alphabet. These letters were A, B, C (pronounced /k/), D, E, F, Z, I, K, L, M, N, O, P, Q, R, S, T, V (V was a vowel pronounced /u/). These letters were similar to those in Semitic, Greek, and Etruscan alphabets. The Romans were very concerned about beauty and symmetry in their writing. This is reflected in the development of rounded visually pleasing versions of the alphabet.

The Romans changed the names of the letter. The names of the vowels reflect the pronunciation, whereas the consonants' names were pronounced with an e sound on either side (be, es, el). Variations developed over time. The letter Z was dropped. The letter C, which had represented voiced and unvoiced variations, was separated. The C was used for unvoiced and the letter G placed in the seventh position represented the voiced version. It is felt that Y and Z were added as Greek loanwords began to assimilate. The letters J, U, and W were added later. The J is a variation of I. Originally the I was used to represent the /e/ phoneme as in [kek]. Over time, the same symbol was used to represent the /j/ phoneme. The letter J was introduced to eliminate confusion. Thus, J sounded like /dʒ/ as in [dʒus].

In Old English, the I was a vowel. In Middle English I became both a consonant and a vowel. The consonantal I sounded like the /dʒ/ sound due to the French influence. The letter J is an outgrowth of cursive writing of the I in and elongated form. During Middle English the letter Y was used as an alternative to the I. For several hundred years I, J, and Y were used interchangeably. (Note this in modern spelling.) The J was used in Roman Numeral IIJ representing 3. The dot on the j and i is a hold over from Middle English slanted line over the I. The slanted line originally was used to differentiate M, N, and U and to differentiate a double I from a U.

In the 17th century, the J was established in English as it is today. In Samuel Johnson's dictionary (1755 A.D.) I and J were still one letter. In Noah Webster's (1806) dictionary they appeared as two letters.

U developed from the Roman V. It was originally an individual interpretation of the V. The V/U were both consonants and vowels and their use was dependent on position in the word. The V was used in initial position and the U in medial and final positions. The use of the letters as today began in the 1700s.

The letter W (double U) was used in the 7th century when the scholars imposed the Latin alphabet on English. In the 8th century, the Runic wynn was used. The use of the W was continued in French. During Middle English it was restored to the alphabet and the wynn was eliminated.

THE PRINTED WORD AND WRITING

Capital Manuscripts

The first type of writing that was used was **capital manuscripts.** These symbols were used on stone, metal, or bone and were ceremonial in nature. These letters were etched or chiseled. The earliest variation of these capitals was majuscule cursive writing.

Majuscule Cursive Writing

Majuscule cursive writing included rounded forms of the earlier letters. This writing was flowing and also allowed the inclusion of ligatures. The use of cursive writing is directly linked to the invention of reed and quill pens to write with and parchment, vellum, and papyrus to write on. Cursive writing can be traced to the Greeks in the 3rd century B.C. and to the Romans in Pompeii in 79 A.D. Cursive writing was used informally until it gained literary acceptance in the 10th century. The capital cursive forms used today are directly from the 10th century.

Lowercase Minuscule Letters

Lowercase or minuscule letters date to Uncial writing in the 3rd century. It was used from the 4th to the 8th centuries and the letters were derivatives of the capital version. Semiuncial writing is a direct outgrowth of unicial writing. The letters were modified as attempts to make the style cursive increased. This style is actually the father of small letters in that all small letters developed from this.

Caroline Minuscule

Caroline minuscule is a variation of the earlier script that according to history, was invented at the end of the 8th century by Alcuin of York who was the abbot and founder of the school of Tours. This script combined majuscules and minuscules. The minuscules were smaller and different in appearance. It was at this time that capital letters were used to begin sentences.

Caroline minuscule was used from the 9th to 23th centuries. Its use waned and Gothic letters were used in the 13th and 14th centuries only to reappear during the Renaissance.

Printing and the Use of Gothic and Roman Types

With the invention of printing, two forms of written English were needed: the printed version and the handwritten version. Gutenberg and his followers chose the Gothic type and used this in all printed material. At the beginning of the 18th century, Roman type, which is an outgrowth of Caroline minuscule, was introduced. This is the print with its many variations that is currently used in printing.

Handwriting

Handwriting continued to use the Caroline minuscule model but became flowery with embellishments. In the early 20th century, the Palmer method was introduced in an effort to make printed and handwritten material more similar. Although the **Palmer method** reduced the flowery, calligraphy aspects of handwriting, anyone learning the language was faced with four variations of each letter. In order to help children assimilate these variations and to boost early reading skills, cursive writing is not introduced until the third or fourth grade in the United States. Today, the **D'Nealian** alphabet is used in many elementary schools. This alphabet is more rounded than the Palmer method alphabet and allows an easier transition to cursive writing while still appearing similar to the printed word.

SPELLING

Spelling During Old English

A variety of spellings were used in Old English writing. Spelling variation is attributed to illiteracy of the Anglo-Saxon people and the use of both the Runic and Roman alphabets. In these early times, English was recorded by scholars and priests who were more familiar with Latin than English. These scholars imposed their alphabet (Roman) on the spoken language in order to record it. Some scholars did use Runic symbols, which lead to further individual variations.

Spelling During Middle English

During Middle English, French was the official language of the country and Latin was the language of scholars. English continued to be used by the middle and low classes but spelling variations were prominent. Spelling variations were influenced by dialectal differences, the maintenance of Old English spellings and the influence of French and Latin scribes.

Reestablishment of English as the Official Language

When English again became the official language in the 13th century, new spelling traditions began. These traditions included tracing the roots of the words and maintaining that spelling. Many words were traced to their Latin origin and the spelling was changed. Some words are neither phonetically correct or historically correct. For example *hiccup* was changed to *hiccough*.

Printing and Its Impact on Spelling

Printing had a major impact on spelling. Although it is believed that the Chinese were using a "printing press" in the 1300s, it was Gutenberg who made printing popular in the west, and Caxton who brought printing to England. It became the practice in printing that books of less importance were printed in the vernacular. Although the original intent was monetary, the printing of books in English helped elevate the importance of the language.

Caxton's Influence on Spelling

During Caxton's time there were four forces influencing spelling: the beginnings of the great vowel shift, the practice of historically tracing word origins and changing spellings to reflect original intent, the scribal tradition of preserving spellings, and dialectal differences. Printers were often scribes who were actually copyists not scholars. They wanted uniform spellings. Caxton, being a copyist, chose to preserve traditional spellings in his printing. His decision had a permanent effect on spelling. Spelling and pronunciation became permanently separated.

Spelling Reformers

Spelling reformers, called **orthoeopists** (one who is concerned with correct spelling), began to appear in the 1500s. Although all orthoeopists were interested in spelling reform, several factions developed. One group wanted to add symbols to the present alphabet, a second group proposed changing spelling to correspond with pronunciation, and the third group was concerned with maintaining consistency in spelling patterns.

The 1600s to 1800s saw the importance of spoken and written language as a socially correct idea established. The idea of an academy to set rules for English spelling and grammar was considered but never established. In order to maintain correctness books on grammar and dictionaries were established.

DICTIONARIES AND THEIR ROLE IN SPELLING REFORM

Glossaries and Other Early Tools

Glossaries date back to the 8th century and represented tools to help young scholars. These glossaries consisted on lists of less common or foreign words and their meanings. Other early tools included vocabularies, teaching manuals, and interlingual dictionaries. Vocabularies were popular from the 10th through 12th century and were used to teach Latin. Words were organized by topic and each word had a Latin and English equivalents. Teaching manuals used in the 16th century were more detailed than vocabularies including methods and techniques for teaching. Interlingual dictionaries were later used to translate and teach languages.

True Dictionaries

English Schoole-Maister, written and compiled by Coote in 1596 A.D., is considered the link between earlier variations and a true dictionary. Coote compiled 1400 A.D. English words and indicated by typeface if the word was Latin, French, or native. He also included definitions of the meaning of each word. Cawdrey published the first true dictionary in 1604 A.D. All words of English origin were explained in English, listed alphabetically and with derivations.

The first attempts at a universal dictionary were made by Kersey in 1708 A.D. and Bailey in 1730 A.D. These volumes included the listing of all words in the English language. Although these dictionaries fell short of their goal, they laid the groundwork for Samuel Johnson.

Johnson's Dictionary

Samuel Johnson's *A Dictionary of the English Language,* written in 1747 A.D., is considered the milestone for all future dictionaries. Johnson's dictionary had two volumes of more than 2,300 pages. This dictionary became the authority on pronunciation and spelling. Many scholars believe Johnson's dictionary represents the final fixation of English spelling.

Oxford English Dictionary

Oxford English Dictionary is considered the most extensive dictionary available for use today. This dictionary first published by the Philogical Society in 1884 under the direction of Sir James Murray was entitled *A New English Dictionary on Historical Principle.* The dictionary lists all words, derivations, and meanings since the 12th century.

AMERICAN SPELLING

Webster's Influence

Noah Webster's influence on spelling in America was very substantial. Webster, born in Connecticut and educated at Yale, was a patriotic individual who reflected this patriotism in compiling these elementary books on English. These books, a spelling book, a grammar book, and a reader became enormously popular. The first part of the series was reissued and entitled *The American Spelling Book*. The eventual outgrowth of this popular volume was *An American Dictionary of the English Language* published in 1828. Prior to Webster's texts, children were still taught using British texts. After the American Revolution, there was a desire to change instruction. Although Webster's own opinions on the changes varied significantly in his various publications, he was instrumental in orchestrating change. His work continues to live on *Webster's Third New International Dictionary* published in 1961 by the Merriam Company.

Other Influences

Noah Webster and Benjamin Franklin worked together to devise *A Scheme for a New Alphabet and a Reformed Mode of Spelling* in 1768. This document proposed changing the alphabet to eliminating the letters C, J, Q, W, X, and Y. In addition, other spelling variations such as *honor* for *honour* were proposed. Although no subsequent changes occurred as a result of this document, many minor spelling changes have become part of American-English.

A board entitled the Simplified Spelling Board was formed in 1906 by Andrew Carnegie. This board suggested about 300 changes including *program* for *programme*. Although their changes were endorsed by Theodore Roosevelt, Congress did not accept them. Some of the changes have been assimilated.

The last attempt at spelling reform in the United States was conducted by Robert McCormack, the editor of *The Chicago Tribune* (1880–1955). He used alternate spellings in the paper for many years. Upon his death, however, traditional spelling was resumed. (For more information, see Bryson, 1991.)

Review Questions

1. What peoples were responsible for the spread of the Semitic alphabet?
2. What was significant about the make-up of the Semitic alphabet?
3. What form of the Greek alphabet became the accepted version?
4. What materials and instruments were used in early Greek writing?
5. List and explain the characters of the Roman alphabet.
6. How did the Romans pronounce the names of the letters?
7. What was the first type of writing?
8. To what is the use of cursive writing directly related?
9. What is another name for lowercase letters?
10. What is Caroline minuscule?
11. What were the two types of print used by early printers?
12. What are the two names associated with handwriting styles currently in use?
13. What can we attribute spelling variations to during Old English?
14. What can we attribute spelling variations to during Middle English?

15. When did English again become the official language?
16. What were the four forces influencing spelling variation during Caxton's time?
17. What is another name for a spelling reformer?
18. What is a glossary? Are glossaries still used today?
19. What do we mean by a true dictionary? What do we mean by a universal dictionary?
20. Who wrote the dictionary that was considered a literary milestone?
21. Why is the *Oxford English Dictionary* considered the ultimate dictionary?
22. Webster exerted influence on American spelling through two books. What are the titles of these books?
23. Choose three others who tried to influence spelling reform and mention their role briefly.

Exercises

1. Trace the history of the letters I, J, Y, U, and V from the Roman alphabet to current use.
2. Where could you find a glossary today?
3. How many volumes are in the *Oxford English Dictionary*?
4. List 10 words that have British and American spellings.
5. List 10 words that have more than one acceptable spelling variation.
6. List 10 words whose spellings have been changed for advertising purposes.

NOTES

Appendix F

Loanwords

1. Transcribe each of the following groups of loanwords into phonetics using stress as appropriate and label the phonological pattern.
2. Do you note any patterns of pronunciation, spelling, or vocabulary in the various groups of loanwords?

Germanic Loanwords

bone	ear
night	calf
ground	star
death	head
world	wise
joy	greed

Celtic Loanwords

clan	loch
bog	plaid
glen	whisky

Scandinavian Loanwords

viking	fellow
urge	ugly

gauntlet	husband
ransack	cross
fiord	they
them	their
noble	scorch
scotfree	take
skywing	sister
since	town
village	skin
skirt	kilt
muggy	rug
freckle	leg
skull	meek
rotten	clasp
crawl	dazzle
scream	trust
scrub	sky
ski	

Latin Loanwords

pauper	proviso
equivalent	legitimate
index	scribe
simile	collect
mediator	opus
ego	referendum

library	simile
paralysis	cancer
extra	anthem
insomnia	bonus
specimen	circus
fulcrum	nucleus
alibi	school
sacrament	nervous
altar	candle
relic	vertebra
nervous	discipline
appendix	pharynx
data	apostle

French Loanwords

choice	cloister
marriage	employ
jury	voyage
royal	justice
felony	market
plaintiff	privilege
traitor	petty
mustache	piquant
machine	parole
prestige	apparel
tongue	physician

attache   ballet

tableau   liaison

damage   forte

decor   penchant

chagrin   reprimand

chauffeur   fiancee

liquor   volume

surprise   surgeon

volley   guardian

Greek Loanwords

graph   phone

atom   character

chorus   cycle

tragedy   tyrant

theatre   phenomenon

zone   diphthong

acrobat   academy

anesthesia   bible

ecstasy   nymph

chorus   larynx

pandemonium   hyphen

pylon   metaphor

kudos   diet

mystery   epigram

electric   theory

chronicle

anemia

agnostic

democracy

rhythm

drama

Italian Loanwords

broccoli

artichoke

arcade

piazza

concerto

spaghetti

prima donna

studio

inferno

violin

alto

lagoon

umbrella

cupola

cupola

volcano

vendetta

dilettante

macaroni

madonna

replica

gondola

lottery

solo

ghetto

studio

replica

piccolo

Spanish Loanwords

renegrade

spade

siesta

mosquito

dagova

canyon

grandee

cannibal

potato

desperado

moose

bronco

rodeo	buffalo
avocado	mustang
stampede	cafeteria
alligator	barbeque
bolero	chocolate
cockroach	cigar
cocoa	plaza
tomato	bonanza

Portuguese Loanwords

| marmalade | buffalo |
| mandarin | caste |

High German Loanwords

pretzel	noodle
eager	sauerkraut
hamburger	zwieback
yodel	nickel
poltergeist	cobalt
hamster	waltz
dachshund	spitz
plunder	eager
pumpernickel	noodle
delicatessen	phooey

Arabic Loanwords

algebra	cipher
saffron	admiral
cotton	amber
arsenal	assassin
alchemy	alcohol
zero	garble
syrup	alcove
gazelle	hashish
harem	almanac
elixir	alkali
hazard	lemon
magazine	coffee

India Loanwords

Nirvana	yoga
karma	dungaree
bungalow	shampoo
dinghy	pagoda

Persian Loanwords

azure	khaki
shawl	bazaar
check	chess
caravan	

Japanese Loanwords

soy	kimono
ricksha	sake
kamikaze	

Chinese Loanwords

tea	silk
catshup	tycoon
judo	

Dutch Loanwords

deck	hoist
buoy	bulwark
loiter	spool
groove	hop (plant)
luck	booze
cruise	knapsack
hobble	splice
dock	drill
hustle	uproar
nitwit	yacht
cookie	caboose

American Indian Loanwords

opposum	skunk
raccoon	hickory
skunk	squash
wigwam	papoose

paleface	warpath
firewater	Indian giver
warpaint	scalp
Great Spirit	pow wow
pecan	totem
caribou	caucas

African Loanwords

voodoo	goober(peanut)
banjo	jigger (sand flea)
cooter(turtle)	

Fronterisms (words associated with the frontier)

johnnycake	showboat
six shooter	homestead
log cabin	pony express
merc (mercantile store)	batter bread

Words that entered American-English after 1900

multistory	storm trooper
carless	cheeseburger
majorette	lovein
sit-in	beatnik
denazify	rubbernecker
smog	nylon
brain drain	sitcom

CD	television
cassette	Rom
yuppie	soundbites
lunar module	foncard
law-abiding	babysitter
joyride	weekend
gadget	fridge
raincheck	carjacking
hijacking	gimmick
bedrock	disc
preppy	flextime
sunblock	emote

See Pyles and Algeo (1993) for additonal loanwords.

NOTES

References

Bryson, B. (1991). *The mother tongue: English and how it got that way.* New York: Avon Books.

Chomsky, N., & Halle, M. (1968). *The sound pattern of English.* New York: Harper & Row.

Creaghead, N. A., Newman, P. W. & Secord, W. A. (1989). *Assessment and remediation of articulatory and phonological disorders* (2nd ed.). Columbus, OH: Merrill.

Faircloth, S. R., & Faircloth, M. A. (1973). *A program of instruction: phonetic science.* Boston: Allyn & Bacon.

Grunwell, P. (1982). *Clinical phonology.* Rockville, MD: Aspen Systems.

Hillenbrand, J., Getty, L., Clark, M., & Wheeler, K. (1995). Acoustic characteristics of American English vowels. *Journal of the Acoustical Society of America, 97,* 3099–3111.

Ingram, D. (1976). *Phonological disability in children.* New York: Elsevier.

International Phonetic Association. (1989). Report on the 1989 Kiel Convention. *Journal of the International Phonetic Association, 19,* 67–80.

Irwin, O. C., & Chen, H. P. (1946). Infant speech: Vowel and consonant frequency. *Journal of Speech Disorders, 11* , 123–125

Khan, L., & Lewis, N. (1986). *Phonological analysis.* Circle Pines: MN: American Guidance Service.

Ladefoged P. (1993). *A course in phonetics* (3rd ed.). Fort Worth, TX: Harcourt Brace Jovanovich College Publishers.

Owens, R. E., Jr. (1996). *Language development* (4th ed.). Boston: Allyn & Bacon.

Palmer, J. M. (1993). *Anatomy for speech and hearing* (4th ed.) Baltimore: Williams & Wilkins.

Palmer, J. M., & Yantis, P.A. (1990). *Survey of communication disorders.* Baltimore: Williams & Wilkins.

Peters, R. A. (1968). *A linguistic history of English.* Boston, MA: Houghton Mifflin.

Peterson, G. E., & Barney, H. L. (1952). Control methods used in a study of the vowels. *Journal of the Acoustical Society of America, 24* , 175–184.

Pullum, G. K. (1990). Remarks on the 1989 revision of the International Phonetic Alphabet. *Journal of the International Phonetic Association, 20,* 33–40.

Pullum, G. K. & Ladusaw, W. A. (1986). *Phonetic symbol guide.* Chicago, IL: University of Chicago Press.

Sander, E. (1972). When are speech sounds learned? *Journal of Speech and Hearing Disorders, 37,* 55–63.

Seikel, J. A., King, D. W., & Drumright, P. G. (1997). *Anatomy and physiology for speech and language.* San Diego: Singular.

Smit, A., Hand, L., Frelinger, J., Bernthal, J. & Bird, A. (1990). The Iowa articulation norms projects and its Nebraska replication. *Journal of Speech and Hearing Disorders, 55,* 779–798.

Woods, H. B. (1990). *Syllable stress & unstress* (Rev. ed.). Ottawa, Canada: Canadian Government Publishing Centre.

Woods, H. B. (1992). *Rhythm & unstress* (Rev. ed.). Ottawa, Canada: Canadian Government Publishing Centre.

Index

Review Questions can be found on the following pages:

9–10, 27–28, 46–47, 57, 74, 83, 98, 110, 119, 137, 143, 165, 187, 206, 215–216, 220, 227–228, 234, 239, 245

Exercises can be found on the following pages:

10, 28, 47–50, 32–43, 52–57, 57–61, 65–74, 74–78, 79–83, 83–85, 85–97, 98–105, 106–110, 110–112, 12–118, 119–129, 137, 143–147, 152–157, 159–161, 165–174, 179–187, 188–202, 206–209, 216–220, 228, 234–235, 239, 245–246, 247–256